My Apple TV®

Sam Costello

que®

800 East 96th Street,
Indianapolis, Indiana 46240 USA

My Apple TV®

Copyright © 2016 by Pearson Education, Inc.

ISBN-13: 978-0-7897-5017-4
ISBN-10: 0-7897-5017-1

Library of Congress Control Number: 2015957575

First Printing: February 2016

Trademarks

Warning and Disclaimer

Special Sales

For information about buying this title in bulk quantities, or for special sales opportunities (which may include electronic versions; custom cover designs; and content particular to your business, training goals, marketing focus, or branding interests), please contact our corporate sales department at corpsales@pearsoned.com or (800) 382-3419.

For government sales inquiries, please contact governmentsales@pearsoned.com.

For questions about sales outside the U.S., please contact intlcs@pearson.com.

Editor-in-Chief
Greg Wiegand

Senior Acquisitions Editor
Laura Norman

Development Editor
Todd Brakke

Managing Editor
Sandra Schroeder

Project Editor
Mandie Frank

Copy Editor
Paula Lowell

Indexer
Cheryl Lenser

Proofreader
The Wordsmithery LLC

Technical Editor
Paul Sihvonen-Binder

Editorial Assistant
Cindy Teeters

Designer
Mark Shirar

Compositor
Tricia Bronkella

Contents at a Glance

	Introduction	1
Chapter 1	Introduction to Your Apple TV	5
Chapter 2	Controlling Your Apple TV: The Remote, Siri, and Search	31
Chapter 3	Using iTunes for TV and Movies	67
Chapter 4	Using Other Video Apps: Netflix, HBO, and More	93
Chapter 5	Using Apps and Games	137
Chapter 6	Music Television: Music on the Apple TV	169
Chapter 7	Advanced TV Topics	211
Chapter 8	Take Control of Your Apple TV's Settings	239
Chapter 9	Troubleshooting Apple TV	265
	Index	287

Table of Contents

Introduction   **1**

    Using This Book 1

1   **Introduction to Your Apple TV**   **5**

    Understanding What the Apple TV Is 5

    What You'll Need 7

        A Fast Internet Connection 7

        High-Definition Television 7

        HDMI Cable 8

        An Apple ID 8

    What You Might Want 10

        Surge Protector 10

        Ethernet Cable 11

        Home Theater System or Soundbar 11

        iPhone, iPad, or iPod touch 12

        iCloud Account 12

        Remote Loop 13

        Game Controllers 14

    Setting Up the Apple TV 14

        Learn the Apple TV's Ports and Connectors 15

        Choose Ethernet vs. Wi-Fi 16

        Connect to a Receiver/Home Theater 17

        Get to Know the Remote Control 17

        Set Up Your Apple TV 20

        Set Up Apple TV Using iPhone or iPad 23

        Get to Know the Apple TV Home Screen 24

        Control Your TV and/or Receiver with the

          Apple TV Remote 26

        Use the Apple TV Remote to Control TV Volume 27

        Use the Remote to Put the Apple TV to Sleep 29

2   **Controlling Your Apple TV: The Remote, Siri, and Search**   **31**

    Using the Remote Control 31

        How to Pair the Remote Control with the Apple TV 33

        Use a Third-Party Remote with Apple TV 34

How to Edit Third-Party Remote Control Settings 36

How to Remove Third-Party Remote Controls 37

The Basics of Using the Remote 38

Use Fast Forward and Reverse 39

How to Control Games 40

Charge the Remote's Batteries 42

How to Tell When Your Battery Is Low 42

How to Connect Bluetooth Headphones to Apple TV 44

How to Connect a Third-Party Game Controller to
      Apple TV 45

Using the Remote App 46

How to Set Up the Remote App 47

How to Use the Remote App 48

Using Siri to Control the Apple TV 50

Activating Siri 50

Frequently Used Siri Commands 51

Searching the Apple TV 56

Universal Search 56

How to Search Using Siri 57

Refine Your Searches 59

Search Using the Search App 60

Anatomy of the Search Results Screen 61

3   **Using iTunes for TV and Movies**   **67**

Renting and Buying Movies at iTunes 67

Search for Movies 68

Browsing Movies 69

Browse Featured Releases 69

Browse By Genre 69

Anatomy of the Movie Detail Screen 71

Rent and Buy Movies 71

Rules for Rentals 73

Watch Movies 74

Learn About the Movie You're Watching 76

Watch Previous iTunes Movie Purchases 77

Turn on Subtitles for Movies and TV 78

Buying TV Shows at iTunes 79

Search for TV Shows 79

Browse TV Shows 80

Buy TV Shows 82

Buy a Season Pass 83

Get New Episodes Via Season Pass 84

Watch TV Shows 84

Watch Previous iTunes TV Show Purchases 87

Using Home Sharing to Watch Movies and TV Shows
from Your Computer 88

Enable Home Sharing 89

Watch Movies and TV Shows Using Home Sharing 90

4 Using Other Video Apps: Netflix, HBO, and More   93

Using Network TV Apps 93

Watch Network TV Apps 94

Network TV Apps with Streaming Services 97

Using Netflix 98

Log In to Your Netflix Account 98

Subscribe to Netflix 99

Search for Movies and TV 101

Add Movies and TV Shows to Your Netflix Queue 102

Remove Movies and TV from Your Netflix Queue 103

Options to Watch and Control Movies and TV Shows
on Netflix 104

How to Rate Content 106

Using HBO 107

Sign In to HBO GO 108

Sign In to HBO NOW 110

Sign Up for HBO NOW 111

Finding Content in HBO Apps 113

Add Items to the Watchlist 114

Options to Watch and Control Movies and TV
on HBO 115

Using Showtime 117

Sign In To Showtime Anytime 117

Sign In To Showtime Streaming 119

Sign Up For Showtime Streaming 120

Finding Content In Showtime Apps 122

Add Items to My List 123

Options to Watch and Control Movies and TV
on Showtime 124

Using Hulu 126

Sign In to Your Hulu Account 126

Subscribe to Hulu 127

Find Content in Hulu 129

Options to Watch and Control Movies and TV Shows
on Hulu 130

Video Apps to Check Out 132

5 Using Apps and Games   137

Finding Apps and Games 137

Search the Apple TV App Store 138

Browse the Apple TV App Store 138

All About the App Detail Screen 140

Downloading and Managing Apps 141

How to Buy Apps 142

Stop Having to Enter Your Password for Every
Download 143

Delete Apps 145

Requesting Refunds for Paid Apps 147

Manage Your Storage 148

Review Apps at the App Store 150

Playing Games on the Apple TV 151

Use the Siri Remote to Play Games 152

Use Third-Party Game Controllers 153

Sign In to Game Center 154

Use Game Center to Check Scores 155

Challenge Friends to Games 156

Use Game Center for Multiplayer Gaming 157

Managing In-App Purchases and Subscriptions 159

Make In-App Purchases 160

Turn Off In-App Purchases 161

Manage Your Subscriptions 162

Updating Apps to New Versions 163
    Enable Automatic App Updates 164
Apps Worth Checking Out 164

6 Music Television: Music on the Apple TV   169

Accessing and Playing Your Music 170
    Access Your iTunes Music Library 170
    Use Your Full iTunes Library on the Apple TV 172
    Browse Your Music Library 173
    Search Your Music Library 175
    Use Siri to Search for Music 176
Using Apple Music 177
    Sign Up for Apple Music 178
    Cancel Apple Music 178
    Add Songs and Albums from Apple Music
        to Your Library 180
    Remove Apple Music Songs or Albums
        from Your Library 182
Listening to Music 184
    Play Your Music 184
    Master the Playback Screen 185
    Favorite Songs 188
    Shuffle Your Music 189
    Use Playlists 192
    Use Sound Check to Equalize Song Volumes 193
Discover New Music in Apple Music 194
    Get Recommendations from Apple with For You ... 195
    Improve the For You Recommendations 196
    Check Out the Latest Releases 196
Tuning In Radio on Your TV 197
    Listen to Beats 1 198
    Enjoy Curated Radio Stations in Your Favorite Genres ... 199
    Create Custom Radio Stations 201
    Modify Your Curated or Custom Radio Stations 203
Using Pandora on Apple TV 205
Music Apps to Check Out 206

7 Advanced TV Topics   **211**

Viewing Photos and Videos on Your Apple TV 211
Sign In to iCloud Photo Stream 212
View Photos and Videos on Your Apple TV 213
Use Apple TV to Display a Slideshow 214
Access Photos on Your Computer Without
Using iCloud 215
Customizing Your Home Screen Layout 217
Change the Home Screen Layout 217
Using Content Restrictions 218
Enable Content Restrictions 219
Manage Content Restrictions 220
Turn Off Content Restrictions 222
Reset Your Password (and Everything Else) 223
Using AirPlay and AirPlay Mirroring 225
Stream Audio from an iPhone or iPad 225
Stream Audio from a Mac 227
Enable AirPlay Mirroring from an iPhone or iPad 229
AirPlay Mirroring from a Mac 230
Configure AirPlay Settings 232
Understanding the Apple TV's Advanced Audio and
Video Settings 233
Change HDMI Output Format 233
Adjust the Apple TV's Output Resolution 234
Calibrate Your Television 235
Change Your Audio Mode 236
Change Your Audio Output 236

8 Take Control of Your Apple TV's Settings   **239**

Setting Your Screensaver 239
Use Apple's Screensavers 240
Use Your Photos as Screensavers 242
Choose How Quickly Screensavers Appear 243
Tweak Your Auto-Sleep Setting 244
Controlling Your Privacy Settings 245
Disable Location Services 245
Control Location Services for Individual Apps 247

Don't Share Diagnostic Data 247
Limit Ad Tracking 249
Customizing Interface Settings 250
Make Onscreen Text Easier to Read 250
Reduce Transparency Effects 251
Enable High-Contrast Focus Style 252
Reduce Animations and Motion 252
Turn Off Navigation Clicks 253
Disable Sound Effects and Music 254
Turn Off Siri 254
Configuring Accessibility Settings 255
Enable Closed Captions 255
Change the Closed Caption Style 256
Create a Custom Closed Caption Style 257
Enable Audio Descriptions 259
Change the Default Subtitle Language 259
Make Apple TV Read Onscreen Text Using VoiceOver ... 260
Make Onscreen Elements Bigger with Zoom 262
Enable Accessibility Shortcut 263

9 Troubleshooting Apple TV   **265**
Restarting the Apple TV 265
Restart the Apple TV Using the Remote 266
Restart the Apple TV Using the Settings App 266
Updating the Operating System 267
Update tvOS Manually 268
Automatically Update tvOS 269
Resetting or Restoring the Apple TV 269
Reset or Restore the Apple TV 270
Backing Up the Apple TV 271
Fixing Problems with Your Account 272
Solve Apple ID Problems 272
Recover a Forgotten Apple ID Password 274
Solving Problems with the Siri Remote 277
Charge the Battery 277
What to Do If the Remote Isn't Working 277

Resolving Internet Connection Issues 278

Check Your Network Connection 278

Reset Your Wireless Router 279

Reset Your Cable Modem 279

Getting Help from Apple 280

Get Help at the Apple Store 281

Get Phone Support from Apple 286

Index   **287**

About the Author

Sam Costello lives in Providence, Rhode Island. He has written about technology, movies, books, comics, and more for magazines and websites including *PC World*, CNN.com, *Rue Morgue*, *Amazing Stories*, and *InfoWorld*.

He previously wrote *My iPad for Kids* (2012) for Que Publishing.

Sam has been the About.com iPhone and iPod Expert since 2007. At that site—http://ipod.about.com—he writes reviews, how-tos, and tech support articles about the iPhone, iPod, iTunes, and other Apple technologies.

In addition to nonfiction, he also writes comics and short stories, including the award-winning horror webcomic *Split Lip*.

By day, Sam is a business analyst in the Boston office of Digitas, a leading digital marketing agency, where he focuses on mobile and innovation projects.

Sam lives with his partner Jenn and their cats, Oni and Clarence. He holds a Media Studies degree from Ithaca College.

Website: http://www.samcostello.net

Twitter: @samcostello

Dedication

This one is for Jenn, who makes me, and everything I do, better.

Acknowledgments

Thanks to everyone at Pearson who helped bring this book to life: Laura Norman, Todd Brakke, Paul Sihvonen-Binder, Mandie Frank, Paula Lowell, Cindy Teeters, and anyone I might be forgetting. It's a pleasure to work with all of you.

We Want to Hear from You!

As the reader of this book, *you* are our most important critic and commentator. We value your opinion and want to know what we're doing right, what we could do better, what areas you'd like to see us publish in, and any other words of wisdom you're willing to pass our way.

We welcome your comments. You can email or write to let us know what you did or didn't like about this book—as well as what we can do to make our books better.

Please note that we cannot help you with technical problems related to the topic of this book.

When you write, please be sure to include this book's title and author as well as your name and email address. We will carefully review your comments and share them with the author and editors who worked on the book.

Email: feedback@quepublishing.com

Mail: Que Publishing
         ATTN: Reader Feedback
         800 East 96th Street
         Indianapolis, IN 46240 USA

Reader Services

Register your copy of *My Apple TV* at quepublishing.com for convenient access to downloads, updates, and corrections as they become available. To start the registration process, go to quepublishing.com/register and log in or create an account*. Enter the product ISBN, 9780789750174, and click Submit. Once the process is complete, you will find any available bonus content under Registered Products.

*Be sure to check the box that you would like to hear from us in order to receive exclusive discounts on future editions of this product.

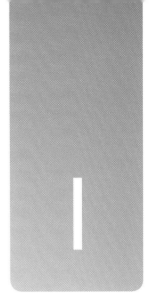

Using This Book

If you've flipped through this book before settling in to read it, you've seen that it uses illustrated step-by-step tutorials to help you learn how to use your Apple TV. Most of those illustrations are screenshots from the Apple TV that match what you'll see when performing the tasks.

One key area in which there are no screenshots is using the Apple TV's remote control. The remote is pretty familiar in most ways—buttons turn on the Apple TV, raise and lower the volume, play or pause video—but there's one big difference: the touchpad at the top. This touchpad is just like the touchpads common on laptops and you use it the same way. Swipe up and down, left and right to move on the Apple TV's screen, just like the mouse pointer on a computer.

Because there are no screenshots for touching the remote, and to make clearer what you should do in those situations, look for small illustrations that show how to move your finger on the touchpad. The basic gestures don't have these illustrations—if you need to move down a list of options, it's pretty clear that you need to swipe down the touchpad. But where things might be less obvious, each illustration includes an arrow indicating which way you should move your finger.

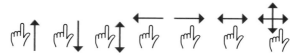

Besides swiping on the touchpad, you can also click. Clicks are used to select menus, apps, and other content.

One of the coolest parts of the Apple TV is that it responds to your voice. Hold down the right button on the remote, speak to the TV, and it obeys you.

There's a lot more in the first few chapters about how to use the remote and the basics of the Apple TV. It might seem daunting now, but it's simple once you've tried it a few times. You'll get the hang of it quickly.

Unlocking the power and fun of the Apple TV starts with setting it up and learning some basic functions.

The Apple TV is a very different way of watching TV shows and movies, playing games, and connecting your living room to the Internet. It's an exciting, powerful, fun tool and there's a lot to learn. In this chapter, you'll find out:

→ What the Apple TV is
→ What you'll need
→ What you might want
→ How to set up Apple TV

Introduction to Your Apple TV

Understanding What the Apple TV Is

The Apple TV looks like a miniature version of your cable box and, just like a cable box, it lets you watch TV shows and movies, but that's where the similarities end.

The Apple TV streams content from the Internet to your living room, whether that content is movies, TV shows, music, games, or even your own photos and videos.

You won't flip through the channels to see what's on because there are no channels, and shows aren't on all the time. That's a good thing. It means that you can choose from a virtually limitless library of movies, TV shows, games, and other content, all just a few taps away, waiting for you whenever you want them.

The Apple TV doesn't replace your cable box. You can have cable and the Apple TV at the same time (that's a good idea, as you'll learn later in this chapter), but you don't need cable. You might choose to join the growing number of "cord cutters," people who no longer subscribe to cable TV and instead get all of their movies and TV over the Internet using services such as Netflix or HBO NOW.

Check For Data Caps

Before you start using your Apple TV too heavily, check the fine print on your Internet service plan. Depending on your provider, your plan, and where you live, there might be a limit on how much you can download each month, after which you'll be charged extra. (These limits are typically set around 300GB.) Streaming movies in HD can require as much as 5GB per movie. If you plan to stream a lot of video, you might want to upgrade your plan or keep an eye on your usage.

Also, it's not just how the content gets to you that has changed. How you find content is different, too. You use a remote that's more like an iPhone than a traditional TV remote control. You can talk to the Apple TV to find something to watch, launch apps, and ask questions—even to play games. In fact, the Apple TV is a lot more like an overgrown iPhone or iPad than traditional TV.

The best way to understand what the Apple TV is, and how it unlocks a whole new world of entertainment, is to start using it.

What You'll Need

After you get your Apple TV, you'll need a few other things to get the most out of it. This section covers items required for setting up and using the device. The later "What You Might Want" section covers things you'll probably want, but that are optional or that you can add later.

A Fast Internet Connection

Because all the content, apps, and games on your Apple TV are delivered over the Internet, make sure you have a very fast Internet connection. This is important not only because it determines how long you have to wait for content to start streaming—no one likes to wait for long downloads—but also because the speed of your Internet connection can determine the quality of the video you get from Netflix and other streaming sources.

You'll also want to decide whether a Wi-Fi or Ethernet connection is best for you, as covered later in the chapter (see "Choose Ethernet vs. Wi-Fi"). For now, just make sure you have speedy Internet service. An Internet plan that offers speeds of 10Mbps or faster should be more than enough to make HD video look great, depending on how many people in your home are simultaneously using it. (That said, the faster the connection you can afford, the better.)

You Need Broadband

The vast majority of people have broadband connections, but some people still use dial up. If you're one of those people, I have bad news: The Apple TV requires broadband. Not only does the box not have a way to connect a dial-up modem, these modems can't deliver fast enough speeds for the content the Apple TV offers.

High-Definition Television

Almost everyone has a high-definition TV these days, but it's worth knowing that having one is a requirement to use the Apple TV. The only connection that the Apple TV has for sending out audio and video signals is HDMI (High-Definition Multimedia Interface). It's right there in the name: HDMI only works with high-def TVs.

It's Not All Good

Sometimes You Need Cable

Although the Apple TV is great for people who love Internet-based services like Netflix and Hulu and don't subscribe to cable, many apps require a valid cable or satellite subscription.

Networks such as ABC, Comedy Central, ESPN, FX, and many others offer a wealth of content in their Apple TV apps, but you can only enjoy that content by signing in to your cable or satellite account to prove that you pay for these channels (blame contracts between cable companies and TV networks for this one).

More and more TV networks are offering their own streaming services that you can subscribe to separately from cable, including HBO and Showtime, but for now, you get the most options and content if you have cable or satellite TV *and* an Apple TV.

HDMI Cable

Connecting the Apple TV and your HDTV means that you need an HDMI cable. The Apple TV doesn't come with one, though, so you'll need to make sure you pick one up before you can start using the device.

Many options are available for HDMI cables. Stay away from the cheapest options—they might not be high quality—but steer clear of the most expensive cables, too. Some companies claim that cables with connectors made out of gold deliver superior audio and video quality and that you should spend $100 or more on their cables. Don't be fooled: Extremely little evidence exists that this is true in most cases. You'll be fine spending $5–$30 on your HDMI cable. Just do some research about good models before you buy: For instance, check Amazon for models that have high average ratings from more than 50 reviewers, and you should be fine.

An Apple ID

If you're already an Apple user on another platform—say the iPhone, iPad, or Mac—you probably have an Apple ID. If this is your first Apple product, don't worry: An Apple ID is free and easy to get.

An Apple ID is an account that you'll use for lots of different things. Want to buy or rent movies at iTunes? You'll use an Apple ID. Interested in signing up for Apple Music? You need an Apple ID to do that. Want to store your photos and videos in the cloud and display them on your Apple TV? I think you know what kind of account you need.

Your Apple ID is also linked to a debit or credit card that you use to pay for things such as movie rentals, apps, and subscriptions. Almost everything you buy on the Apple TV uses your Apple ID.

Get to Know iCloud

Another major account that comes up a lot in this book is iCloud. iCloud is Apple's free online service for storing and syncing your data across multiple devices. Songs, photos, app purchases, and lots of other kinds of data are stored in your iCloud account. Items get into iCloud from virtually any Apple device—an Apple TV, an iPhone or iPad, or a Mac. More information about iCloud appears later in this chapter.

Create an Apple ID

If you already have an Apple ID, sign in to it on your Apple TV to connect this device to all of your others. If you don't have one, follow these steps to set one up:

1. In a web browser on your computer or mobile device, go to https://appleid.apple.com/account. Fill out the form on this website to create your Apple ID account.

2. Use your email address for the Apple ID login. Make sure to take note of the security questions you create. You'll need to remember those to change or reset your Apple ID.

3. After you fill out the form, click Create Apple ID to set up your account.

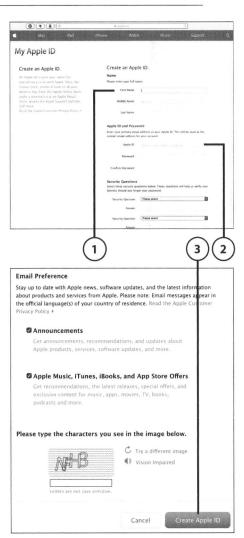

What You Might Want

You now know what's required for using your Apple TV, but some optional items might make using it a lot more enjoyable.

Surge Protector

You've invested hundreds of dollars, or maybe thousands, into your TV, sound system, and Apple TV. Protect that investment with a surge protector. Electrical surges caused by lightning striking your home, flaws in your home's wiring, or other unexpected electrical events can seriously damage electronics, but surge protectors can help protect against damage.

Surge protectors sit between your power outlets and your devices and, when they detect a major surge of electricity, reduce the surge to safer levels. Different models reduce the surge by different amounts, so the more reduction you can get, the better.

Just like with HDMI cables, some manufacturers charge hundreds for a surge protector, but you don't need to pay that. You can get a great model for $20–$40.

For some in-depth research and recommendations, check out http://thewirecutter.com/reviews/best-surge-protector/.

Ethernet Cable

If you choose to connect your Apple TV to the Internet using Ethernet (instead of Wi-Fi), then you'll need an Ethernet cable. It connects the device to your cable modem or router. If you have a desktop PC at work, this is probably the way it gets online.

You can get a good Ethernet cable for under $10, but read the section "Choose Ethernet vs. Wi-Fi" later in this chapter before you buy. You might not need one.

Home Theater System or Soundbar

The speakers built in to most HDTVs are adequate, but that's all they are. To get the most enjoyment out of all the content your Apple TV delivers—especially movies, sports, and games, to say nothing of music—you should consider upgrading your living room sound system.

The less expensive option is a soundbar, a device about the width of an HDTV that contains multiple speakers. It offers sound approaching the quality of a home theater system without the hassle of multiple components and tangles of wires. If you have limited space, aren't a fanatic about sound quality, or just prefer simplicity, a soundbar might be a good choice for you. Expect to spend between $250 and $1,800.

A home theater system, on the other hand, is a good choice if you want the full theater experience of hearing different sounds coming from different parts of the room and having multiple components, each dedicated to a specific kind of sound. With a home theater system, you'll buy a receiver and then connect three, six, or even more speakers to it, including a dedicated subwoofer for deep bass. Home theaters are more expensive and—unless you ante up for wireless models—require running speaker cable throughout your living room, but they deliver great audio. Expect to spend anywhere from $700 to several thousand.

iPhone, iPad, or iPod touch

An iPhone, iPad, or iPod touch—devices you might already have—can be nice accessories for three reasons:

- **Integration**—Apple's mobile devices are tightly integrated with the Apple TV. From apps to iCloud, from your Apple ID to shared photos, from your music to movies, content you create and use on your mobile device can also be used on your Apple TV. Having more than one Apple device allows you to enjoy your content and apps everywhere.

- **Game controller**—Players can use the iPhone as a game controller with some games. It might not be quite as good as a controller dedicated to gaming, but it will save you some money. The iPhone can't control every game on the Apple TV—compatibility is up to the game's developer—but it should come in handy.

- **Remote control**—With Apple's free Remote app, your iOS device can transform into a remote control for the Apple TV. The Remote app doesn't offer all the features that the Apple TV's remote does—for instance, it doesn't support Siri for voice commands—but it's a nice option and makes it easier to type in usernames and passwords.

iCloud Account

Apple's online service for storing your data, iCloud, is a nice add-on to the Apple TV. If you already have other Apple products, you're probably already using iCloud.

In the case of the Apple TV, having an iCloud account lets you display your photos and videos on your HDTV. It's a free account, so if you take a lot of photos, it's worth having. Every iCloud user gets 5 GB of storage for free. If you need more—and you probably will if you take a lot of photos, back up data there, or use it to store content from other Apple devices—you can upgrade. Upping your storage limit to a hefty 50 GB only costs $0.99/month.

Check out "Viewing Photos and Videos on Your Apple TV" in Chapter 7, "Advanced TV Topics," for more on setting up and using iCloud with the Apple TV.

Remote Loop

Remember when Nintendo released its Wii game console, which included a small remote control that you would swing through the air to control games, and how so many people worried about accidentally throwing the remote through their TVs while playing? The same concern will probably crop up with the Apple TV.

That's because you can use the remote that comes with it to play games. Just flip the remote sideways and you're ready to play. The remote senses how you move it and translates that into actions in games, which means you'll be swinging and moving it a lot. Get too into the action and the remote might interact with your TV in a way you don't like.

The Remote Loop, an accessory Apple sells for $13, plugs into the Lightning port at the bottom of the remote, tethers it to your wrist and keeps the remote from sailing through the air. If you have kids who will be playing with the Apple TV, or have a history of klutziness, it's a worthwhile investment.

Game Controllers

The huge library of great games on the iPhone and iPad is likely to make its way to the Apple TV. Although the remote control will work for some, serious gamers will prefer an Xbox- or PlayStation-style game controller. Look for controllers with the MFi (Made for iPhone) certification.

Game Support

According to Apple, the tvOS operating system that runs on the Apple TV is 95% identical to the iOS that runs on iPhones and iPads. That should make porting games to the Apple TV relatively easy for game developers.

Setting Up the Apple TV

We're almost to the really good stuff: using your Apple TV. Before you can do that, you need to set it up. Luckily, the set-up process is pretty quick. Race through these steps and you can start enjoying your Apple TV.

Learn the Apple TV's Ports and Connectors

The Apple TV has a surprisingly small number of ports and connectors. Here's what they do:

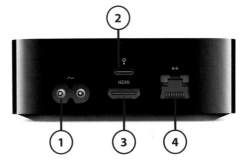

1. **Power supply**—Plug the included power cable in here.

2. **USB-C**—You probably won't use this port. It's a next-generation version of the USB ports that we're familiar with from computers and other devices. As of now, there's nothing to plug into it; it's just there for Apple to connect to in case your Apple TV needs a repair.

3. **HDMI**—Connect the HDMI cable here and plug the other end either directly into one of your TV's HDMI ports or, if you're using a home theater system, plug it into one of the HDMI ports on your receiver.

4. **Ethernet**—Ethernet is one of the ways the Apple TV can connect to the Internet (the other is Wi-Fi). If you choose this approach, you'll connect your Ethernet cable here and plug the other end into your cable modem or router. The next section helps you decide whether Ethernet or Wi-Fi is best for you.

>>>Go Further

UNDER THE HOOD

You'll also use a few things that you can't see because they're internal only:

- **A8 processor**—The brain of the Apple TV is the A8, the same processor that's used by the iPad Air 2 and the iPhone 6. The A8 packs desktop computer–level performance into a tiny package, so you can be sure that the Apple TV is plenty powerful.

- **Memory**—Depending on which model you bought, the Apple TV offers 32 GB or 64 GB of space to store your apps, purchases, rentals, music, and more.

- **Bluetooth**—For connecting the remote, game controllers, and other accessories.

- **An IR (infrared) port**—Used with traditional, third-party remote controls that communicate via IR instead of Bluetooth.

- **Wi-Fi**—For connecting to the Internet wirelessly.

Choose Ethernet vs. Wi-Fi

When setting up your Apple TV, you need to decide how you want to connect it to the Internet so it can download all the great movies, TV shows, games, and apps you enjoy. You have two choices: Ethernet or Wi-Fi.

- **Ethernet**—A cable that connects to your cable modem or router.

- **Wi-Fi**—A wireless networking technology that cuts the cables.

Both options are good for delivering high-definition video to you over the Internet. Wired solutions are often the most reliable (and usually the fastest), but if you have the right equipment, Wi-Fi can be far more convenient and plenty fast.

To get top-speed Wi-Fi, your router needs to support the 802.11ac standard (check the manufacturer's website for information about your router), although an 802.11n router (like those provided by many major cable Internet providers) is adequate. Other factors that go into this decision include whether you have Wi-Fi signal interference problems in your home, whether you have Wi-Fi at all, and whether your Internet connection is relatively slow—but all things being equal, Wi-Fi is often the simplest solution.

Connect to a Receiver/Home Theater

If you have a home theater system or soundbar, I strongly recommend connecting your Apple TV to it. When you do that, you'll get all the benefits of your
speakers and subwoofer when watching movies and TV and playing games. If
you connect the device directly to your TV, you'll have to rely on your TV's (probably lower-quality) speakers.

Setting this up is easy. If your receiver is already connected to your TV, just plug
the Apple TV's HDMI cable into an available HDMI port on your receiver. (If the
port has a label, like HDMI 1 or HDMI 2, make sure to take note of it.)

Now, turn everything on, change the input feed on your receiver to the HDMI
port you plugged the Apple TV into and you should see—and hear—your
Apple TV on your home theater.

Get to Know the Remote Control

Before you can use the Apple TV, you need
to get familiar with what its remote control
can do. Some aspects of the remote will be
familiar from almost any other remote, but
you might encounter other features for the
first time.

1. **Touchpad**—The whole top of the
   remote is a touchpad, just like the
   touchpads that are common on
   most laptops. Swipe up and down, or
   left and right to navigate onscreen.
   Swiping left and right can also rewind
   and fast forward movies and TV. Click
   the touchpad to select an option.

2. **Microphone**—The small hole at the
   top of the touchpad is one of the
   remote's two microphones (the other
   is in the same place on the back side).
   This picks up your voice when you
   speak to the TV, but forget holding
   the remote up to your mouth when
   you speak; this mic is very sensitive
   and powerful, so just speak normally.

3. **Menu button**—When you're using the apps on the TV and want to go back a screen, press the Menu button. If you're in an app and confused about how you got where you are, try the Menu button first. It's often the easiest path out of confusion.

4. **Home button**—Next to the Menu button is a button that looks like a TV; this is the Apple TV's Home button. It gets you back to the Apple TV's main screen with one touch. The Home button also lets you access recently used apps; check out "Go Further: Double-Click the Home Button to Access Recent Apps" in Chapter 2, "Controlling Your Apple TV: The Remote, Siri, and Search," to learn how to do that.

5. **Siri button**—The button with the microphone icon activates Siri. Whenever you want to talk to your TV—to search, ask a question, or control an app or game—press this button first.

6. **Play/Pause button**—To start a movie, song, or TV show playing, or pause it after it's already playing, press this button.

7. **Volume**—Everyone knows what a volume button does. But did you know that if you've configured your Apple TV to also control your TV or home theater receiver, this button adjusts their volume, too? Check out "Control Your TV and/ or Receiver with the Apple TV Remote" later in this chapter for instructions on how to set this up.

8. **IR port**—The remote uses Bluetooth to control the Apple TV itself, but not all TVs have Bluetooth. Many, especially older models, work with traditional remote controls via infrared. Because the Siri Remote lets you adjust the volume on your TV, it needs this infrared port, which you can't quite see in this picture, to make sure it can control virtually any TV.

9. **Accelerometer and gyroscope**—You'll never see these sensors, but if you play games on the Apple TV, you'll use them. The accelerometer tracks the speed at which you move the remote, while the gyroscope understands how you're holding and tilting it. When you use the remote as a game controller, these sensors translate your movements into actions in the game. (Not pictured)

10. **Recharging port**—You can't see it in this photo, but there's a Lightning port at the bottom of the remote (Lightning is the same kind of connector located on the bottom of the iPhone). Use this port to recharge the remote. You also plug in the Remote Loop here.

Set Up Your Apple TV

Now that you know your Apple TV's hardware, it's time to get started using it. With your Apple TV connected to your TV and everything powered on, follow these steps to set it up and dive into the really good stuff:

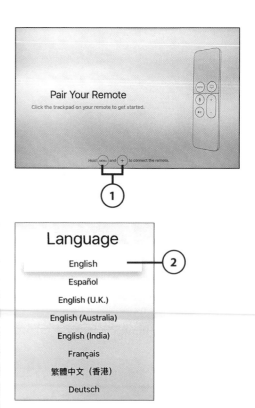

1. When the Apple TV starts up for the first time, it might ask you to connect the remote control. You need to do this to continue the set-up process. To do that, press the Menu and + buttons on the remote at the same time. In a moment, the remote connects to the Apple TV.

No Picture

If you don't see any picture on your TV, and have properly connected Apple TV to your setup, make sure your TV or home theater receiver (or soundbar) is set to the correct video input.

2. Use the remote to highlight your choice of language and click the touchpad to select it.

3. Use the touchpad to select the country or region in which you'll use the Apple TV.

4. Choose how to set up the device—using an iPhone or iPad or manually. For more about using an iPhone or iPad, check out the next section in this chapter. Select Manually using the remote control and continue to step 5.

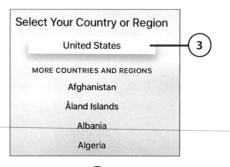

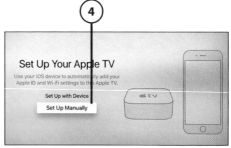

5. Select your home Wi-Fi network from the list of detected Wi-Fi signals. If you protect your Wi-Fi network with a password, enter it here. At this point, your Apple TV connects to Apple's servers and activates itself. This usually takes a few seconds.

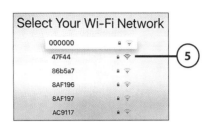

If You're Using Ethernet

If you're using Ethernet to connect your Apple TV to the Internet, you won't need to select a Wi-Fi network. Skip to step 6.

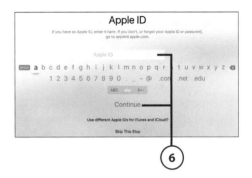

6. Log in to your Apple ID. Remember, doing this is crucial because it gives you access to the iTunes and App Stores, Apple Music, iCloud, and much more. Use the remote to type in your username and then click Continue. Then do the same for your password and tap Continue.

7. Choose whether you want to enable Location Services. This feature enables the Apple TV to know where it's located geographically and provides you content based on that, such as your local weather or sports scores. It's not a requirement, but it's a nice add on.

8. Select whether you want to use Siri. Given that many of the best features of the Apple TV involve talking to Siri, enabling this option is a no brainer.

9. Choose whether you want to use Apple's exclusive new screensavers. These are full-screen, high-definition, and very appealing screensavers. They're updated monthly, but do eat up storage space.

10. Select whether you want to share diagnostic information about performance and app crashes with Apple. No personally identifiable information is shared.

11. Choose if you want to share data about your app usage with the developers of the apps you use. Again, no personal information is shared.

12. Choose Agree when asked to agree to the Terms and Conditions of the Apple TV and its software. To continue using the device, you must agree, so simply highlight Agree and click the touchpad to select it.

And with that, setup is complete. Your Apple TV's home screen appears, where it's time to start the fun.

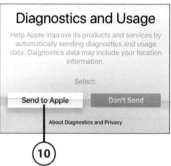

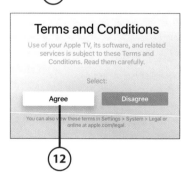

Set Up Apple TV Using iPhone or iPad

As mentioned in the previous tutorial (step 4), you can also set up the Apple TV using your iPhone or iPad. This option can save you a lot of time by copying information your iOS device already has to your Apple TV, reducing the number of setup steps.

Bluetooth Required

To use this setup feature, you need an iPhone or iPad running iOS 9.1, with Bluetooth turned on. If you have that and want to try setting up your Apple TV with it, follow these steps.

1. Highlight Set Up with Device and click the touchpad to select that option.

2. Follow the onscreen instructions: Unlock your iPhone or iPad (that is, wake it up and go to the home screen); turn on Bluetooth; and place the device near your Apple TV so it can detect it.

3. A pop-up window on your iOS device asks whether you want to set up your Apple TV using the device. Tap Continue.

4. Sign in to your Apple ID on the iOS device. This not only adds your Apple ID to the Apple TV, but also signs in to your iCloud and iTunes Store accounts on the TV.

5. Tap OK to continue.

Set Up Your Apple TV

Use your iOS device to automatically add your Apple ID and Wi-Fi settings to this Apple TV.

Set Up with Device ①

Set Up Manually

Requires iOS 9.1 or later.
Not available on iPad 2.

Set Up Your Apple TV

1 Unlock your iOS Device

2 Enable Bluetooth ②

3 Hold device close to the Apple TV

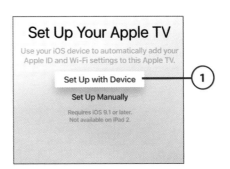

Set Up Apple TV?

Do you want to set up your Apple TV now?

Cancel   Continue ③

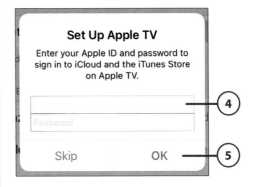

Set Up Apple TV

Enter your Apple ID and password to sign in to iCloud and the iTunes Store on Apple TV.

④

Password

Skip   OK ⑤

6. Choose whether or not to send diagnostic data about your Apple TV to Apple. Tap No Thanks to prevent this or OK to agree.

7. At this point, you'll select the same options as in the manual set up from the previous task—Location Services, Siri, Screensavers, Diagnostics, App Analytics, and Terms and Conditions. For more information on each step, return to step 7 in the previous tutorial.

Get to Know the Apple TV Home Screen

Whichever option for setting up the Apple TV you used, once the process is complete, you come to the device's home screen. You'll spend a lot of time on this screen, so it helps to understand what each item on the screen is and what it does.

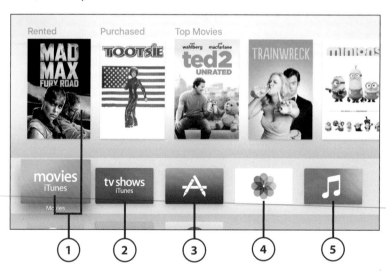

1. **iTunes Movies**—To rent and buy movies from the iTunes Store, use this app. When you highlight the app, the row of images above it changes to show movies you've purchased or rented, as well as top titles from Apple (each app in the top row features similar previews when you highlight it).

2. **iTunes TV Shows**—Just like the iTunes Movies app, except you use this to get TV shows. Learn about both of these apps in depth in Chapter 3, "Using iTunes for TV and Movies."

3. **App Store**—Expand the functionality and fun of your Apple TV by installing apps from the store. You can get streaming apps like Netflix and Hulu, TV network apps from ABC and NBC, or all kinds of games and entertainment apps. Learn about the App Store in Chapter 5, "Using Apps and Games."

4. **Photos**—Display photos from your iCloud Photo Library using this app. Chapter 7 explains some of the major uses of this app.

5. **Music**—The Apple TV isn't just about video. Thanks to this app, it's also full of great music. Use it to access your iCloud Music Library or Apple Music. Chapter 6, "Music Television: Music on the Apple TV," features an extensive set of music-related tutorials.

6. **Search**—This built-in app does the same thing as searching by voice using Siri.

7. **Computers**—If you want to use Home Sharing to access content stored on your Mac or PC, this is the app you need. For more on Home Sharing, check out "Using Home Sharing to Watch Movies and TV" in Chapter 3.

8. **Settings**—Use this app to control preferences and settings related to almost everything you can do on the Apple TV. From restricting mature content from kids to calibrating the Apple TV for your TV and beyond, you'll find it here and discussed throughout this book.

9. **Third-Party Apps**—These are apps you download from the App Store. You won't have any of these when you first set up the Apple TV. Rearrange the position of these apps on the screen by following the instructions in Chapter 7's "Customizing Your Home Screen Layout."

Control Your TV and/or Receiver with the Apple TV Remote

Depending on what kind of TV you have, you can control your TV and home theater receiver from your Apple TV remote; there is no need for expensive all-in-one remotes. Not every TV will work—you need one that supports HDMI-CEC technology.

If your TV offers HDMI-CEC, follow these steps to enable your Apple TV remote to control it:

1. Launch the Settings app from the main menu screen.

2. Select Remotes and Devices.

3. In the Home Theater Control section, select Control TVs and Receivers so that it toggles to On.

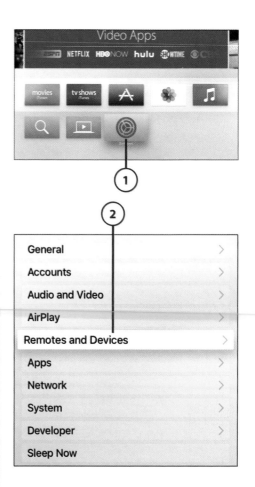

>>>*Go Further*

HDMI-CEC SUPPORT

HDMI-CEC, or Consumer Electronics Control, is a technology that lets components control each other, and one remote can operate up to 15 devices. HDMI-CEC is included in most new TVs, but only in some older ones.

Look for HDMI-CEC under names like Anynet+ (Samsung TVs), Aquos Link (Sharp), BRAVIA Link and BRAVIA Sync (Sony), Kuro Link (Pioneer), INlink (Insignia), CE-Link and Regza Link (Toshiba), SimpLink (LG), and VIERA Link (Panasonic).

Use the Apple TV Remote to Control TV Volume

Even if you don't have a home theater system and just use your TV's built-in speakers, you can still use the Apple TV's remote to control your TV's volume. Just follow these steps:

1. Launch the Settings app.

2. Select Remotes and Devices.

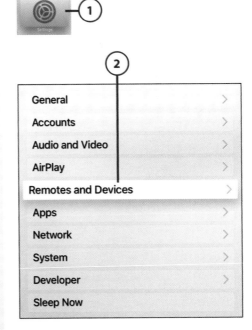

3. In the Home Theater Control section, select Volume Control.

4. On the Select Volume Control screen, choose your preference.

>>>Go Further
CHOOSING A CONTROL TYPE

Choose Auto to automatically detect the best way to control volume for your TV/audio system (if you don't know what you need, pick this); choose Receiver via IR if the audio from your Apple TV is sent through your receiver or soundbar and you control your receiver with infrared; choose TV via IR if your Apple TV is connected directly to your TV and you control your TV with infrared; choose Off to not use your Apple TV remote to control volume.

Use the Remote to Put the Apple TV to Sleep

Your Apple TV automatically goes to sleep—that is, turns itself to a very low-power mode—after a pre-defined period of time. You can also put it to sleep as soon as you're done using it by following these steps:

1. Hold down the Home button on the remote.

2. The screen that appears offers two options: Cancel (if you've changed your mind or held the button down accidentally) or Sleep. Use the touchpad to high-light your choice.

3. Click the touchpad to confirm your choice.

If you want to wake the Apple TV up again, simply press any button on the remote and it springs awake right away.

Power Options

For more on controlling Apple TV sleep mode settings, check out "Tweak Your Auto-Sleep Setting" in Chapter 8, "Take Control of Your Apple TV's Settings."

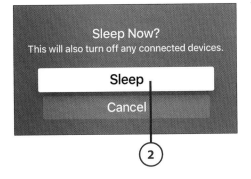

The Apple TV offers a powerful and intuitive new set of ways to
control your TV, including speaking to it.

Controlling the Apple TV is both similar to any other TV and totally, radically different. When you master the controls, you'll start to unlock the fun and power of the device. In this chapter, you'll learn about:

→ Using the remote control
→ Using the Remote app
→ Using Siri to control the Apple TV
→ Searching the Apple TV

2

Controlling Your Apple TV: The Remote, Siri, and Search

The most fun thing about regular TVs is getting to the content. On the Apple TV, the content is equally great, but using the TV—navigating the screen, finding the content—is a lot of fun, too.

Using the Remote Control

Everyone who has used a TV has used a remote control. Some are simple—just a few buttons—whereas others look as complicated as something used to send missions to the moon in the 1960s. It's a safe bet that most people have never used a remote like the one that comes with the Apple TV.

That remote, officially dubbed the Siri Remote by Apple, gives you new and more powerful ways to interact with the TV than ever before.

The three major ways that the Apple TV's remote control differs from other TV remotes are:

- **Voice**—People have been talking back to their TVs for decades, but only in recent years have TVs been able to respond—and even then sometimes in limited ways. With the Apple TV, speaking into the microphone on the remote can control almost every aspect of the TV using Siri. Forget searching the remote for the right buttons or navigating through levels and levels of menus. Just say what you want and the remote helps make it happen.

- **Bluetooth**—Traditional remote controls use infrared technology to control the TV. That means that the remote has to be pointed at the TV's infrared port and that there can't be anything between them to block the signal. That's not the case with the Siri Remote. Because it connects to the Apple TV using Bluetooth, after the connection is established, not only do you not need to point the remote at the TV, you don't even need to be in the same room for it to work (though it's worth noting that Bluetooth's range is limited to around 30 feet).

- **Touch**—The Siri Remote isn't the first TV remote with a touchpad, but it might be the best. Apple is widely acknowledged to make the best touchpads on laptops and it revolutionized computing when it created the multitouch technology that powers the screens on the iPhone and iPad. It's taken that same expertise and attention to detail and applied it to this touchpad to create a smooth and intuitive experience.

Remember, you can get an explanation of what all the buttons on the remote do back in "Get to Know the Remote Control" in Chapter 1, "Introduction to Your Apple TV."

How to Pair the Remote Control with the Apple TV

You connected the remote control to the Apple TV, using a process called pairing, as one of the very first steps in setting up the TV. But if your remote loses its connection or you get a new remote, you'll need to pair it again. In that case, follow these steps (these are for the official Apple remote only; if you want to connect a third-party remote, check out the next section):

1. Put your remote within about three inches of your Apple TV.

2. Point the remote at the front of the Apple TV.

3. Hold down the Menu and Volume Up buttons at the same time.

4. A message on the screen appears to let you know your remote is paired. You can stop pressing the buttons and start using the remote.

Use a Third-Party Remote with Apple TV

The Siri Remote that comes with the Apple TV is versatile and innovative, but it won't match everyone's preference—especially if you've invested hundreds of dollars in an all-in-one remote that controls your home theater and audio systems. If you prefer to use your own remote, you don't need a remote designed for the Apple TV. Any remote that connects using Bluetooth or infrared and that can be programmed works.

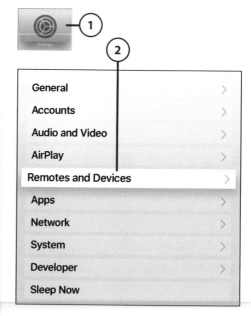

1. Launch the Settings app.

2. Select Remotes and Devices.

3. Select Learn Remote.

4. Next, the Apple TV advises you to select an unused device setting on your remote control that you can add the Apple TV to. Select Start to continue.

5. To set up the remote to control the Apple TV, press the button on the remote that matches the button shown on the screen. This maps the physical buttons to the functions on the device. Hold each button down until the progress bar is complete. Follow all the steps.

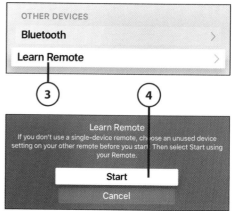

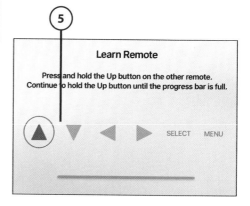

6. With the buttons mapped, next you need to give the new remote control a name. Use the onscreen keyboard to enter a name and then select Done to save it.

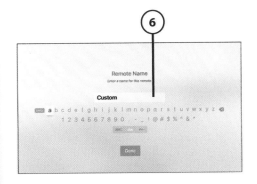

7. The initial set up is now complete. You can either start using the new remote by selecting OK or map other buttons on the remote to other features by selecting Set Up Playback Buttons.

8. If you selected Set Up Playback Buttons, follow the same steps as you did in step 5 (using a different set of buttons on the remote; this works best if you have a universal remote with tons of buttons).

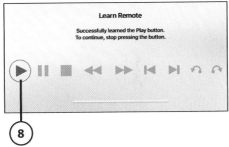

9. When you've completed those steps, select OK to finalize the set up.

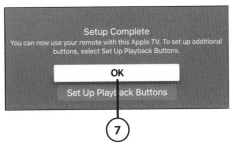

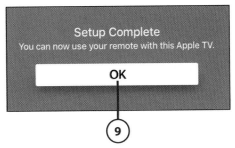

How to Edit Third-Party Remote Control Settings

If you've already set up a third-party remote and mapped its buttons to the functions of the Apple TV, you might find that you want to change some of those settings. Follow these steps to do that:

1. Launch Settings.

2. Select Remotes and Devices.

3. In the Learned Remotes section, select the remote that you want to edit.

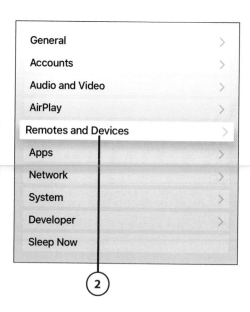

General	>
Accounts	>
Audio and Video	>
AirPlay	>
Remotes and Devices	>
Apps	>
Network	>
System	>
Developer	>
Sleep Now	

LEARNED REMOTES

| Learn Remote | > |
| Custom | |

4. The next screen offers five options: Change the name of the remote; change the setup of the basic buttons (as in step 5 of the last tutorial); change the setup of the playback buttons (step 7 of the last tutorial); delete the remote; or cancel without making changes. Make your selection and follow the onscreen prompts.

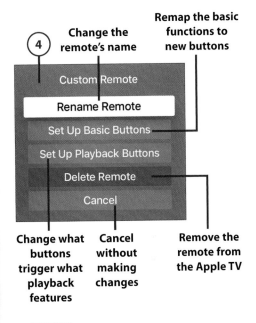

Remap the basic functions to new buttons

Change the remote's name

Change what buttons trigger what playback features

Cancel without making changes

Remove the remote from the Apple TV

How to Remove Third-Party Remote Controls

If you decide you no longer want to use the third-party remote control you set up on your Apple TV, no problem. Remove it by doing this:

1. Launch Settings.

2. Select Remotes and Devices.

3. In the Learned Remotes section, select the remote that you want to edit.

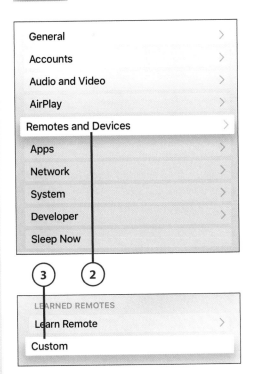

4. Select Delete Remote.

5. Confirm that you want to remove this remote by selecting the Delete Remote button again.

When you do that, the settings for this remote are removed and you're returned to the Remotes and Devices screen, which no longer lists this remote. You'll need to either set up a new one or use the Apple TV's remote.

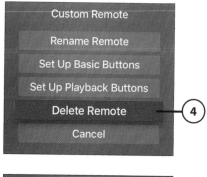

The Basics of Using the Remote

Some of the remote control's most basic and most frequently used features have already been covered, including swiping to move on the screen and tapping to select items. In the following sections are some less obvious, but equally useful, things you can do with the remote.

>>>Go Further

ADJUST THE RESPONSIVENESS OF THE TOUCHPAD

Do you feel like the onscreen cursor is moving through glue when you swipe across the touchpad? Change how quickly it moves so it can keep up with you. The touchpad is set to a moderate speed by default, but you can make it faster or slower. Just go to Settings -> Remotes and Devices -> Touch Surface Tracking and change the speed.

Use Fast Forward and Reverse

The touchpad on the remote makes time scrubbing (a fancy name for fast forwarding and reversing audio and video) simple: Just swipe across the touchpad while the video is playing.

Swipe right to left on the touchpad to move backward in a movie, TV show, or song

Swipe left to right on the touchpad to move forward

The speed of your swipe determines the speed of the time scrubbing. Which-ever direction you're moving, preview images pop up onscreen so you can see where in the video you are. Just click the touchpad when you see the pre-view frame you want to jump to and Apple TV takes you there.

Wiggle on the Touchpad for 3D Effects

One of the fun things about the Apple TV is the cool animations and effects that catch the eye and make onscreen elements seem a little more alive. One of those effects makes things like movie posters and album covers appear to be 3D when you move them. To get a glimpse of this effect, highlight an item on the home screen (this also works in some apps, but it's easiest to see at first on the home screen). Touch your finger to the touchpad without clicking it. Then wiggle your finger back and forth while still touching the touchpad. You should see the item you highlighted move and some three-dimensional depth. It can be tricky to do at first—it's easy to accidentally scroll side to side—but after you have it down, it adds some pizzazz to the Apple TV.

How to Control Games

If you want to play games on your Apple TV, the remote doubles as a game controller. Flip it sideways and—thanks to the touchpad, accelerometer, and gyroscope—you're ready to play. For full details on using the remote as a game controller, check out "Use Third-Party Game Controllers" in Chapter 5, "Using Apps and Games."

A Long-Lasting Battery

It's good to know how to charge the batteries on the remote control, but you probably won't have to do it very often. According to Apple, a full charge of the battery should last around three months.

>>>Go Further

DOUBLE-CLICK THE HOME BUTTON TO ACCESS RECENT APPS

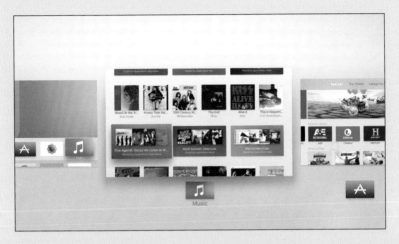

Here's a neat shortcut that you'll start using all the time after you know it. Quickly double-click the Home button on the remote and the Apple TV displays all the apps you've used recently. Swipe between them with the touchpad and when you find one you want to jump to, just click the touchpad. Now, getting to your favorite apps is even faster. If you have an iPhone or iPad, you probably already know how useful this feature is.

Charge the Remote's Batteries

When the battery in your remote is running low, recharging it is easy. Just follow these steps:

1. Plug the Lightning end of the cable that came with the Apple TV into the Lightning port at the bottom of the remote.

2. Plug the other end of the cable into a USB port on a computer or a wall power adapter.

3. The battery should take about nine hours to fully recharge.

It's Not All Good

The Remote's Batteries Can't Be Replaced

Unlike many remote controls that run on standard AA batteries, the Apple TV remote control uses a rechargeable battery. But you won't find any opening on the remote where the battery can be replaced. That's fine when your remote's battery is working well, but if it needs to be replaced, you're out of luck: End users can't replace the battery. For that, you'll need to go to Apple and pay them to do it.

How to Tell When Your Battery Is Low

If your remote control isn't responding as quickly as it used to when you use it, or if it feels like some of the commands you send with it just aren't getting to the Apple TV, the problem could be that its battery is low. Find out whether your remote needs a recharge this way:

1. Launch the Settings app.

2. Highlight Remotes and Devices and click the touchpad.

3. In the Other Devices section, select Bluetooth.

4. On the next screen, the first item is your remote control. The amount of charge its battery has is shown as an icon on the right. A full gray battery icon indicates a 100% charged remote.

Having Problems with the Remote?

If the remote control isn't working properly, don't despair. Check out "Solving Problems with the Siri Remote" in Chapter 9, "Troubleshooting Apple TV," for troubleshooting tips.

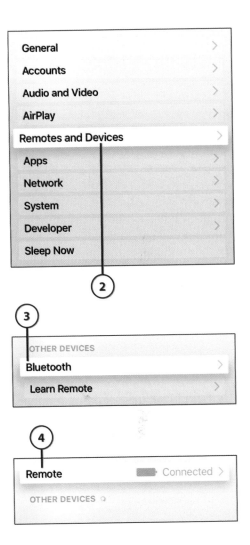

How to Connect Bluetooth Headphones to Apple TV

Have you ever wanted to relax by watching a movie or playing a game while elsewhere in your apartment or home someone is trying to sleep or needs silence? The Apple TV solves this problem thanks to its support of Bluetooth headphones. You just need to connect wireless headphones to the Apple TV and you can enjoy all the content you want without sound coming out of the speakers and disturbing anyone else. Here's how you do it:

1. Put your Bluetooth headphones into pairing mode (not pictured; consult the manual or manufacturer's website for more details).

2. On the Apple TV, launch the Settings app.

3. Select Remotes and Devices.

4. Select Bluetooth.

5. Select your headphones when they appear in the Other Devices menu.

6. When your headphones connect to your Apple TV, they move to the My Devices section and indicate that they are connected.

After you complete these steps, the audio output defaults to the headphones, rather than the TV's speakers. To change the audio output to something else, either turn off the headphones or check out "Change Your Audio Output" in Chapter 7, "Advanced TV Topics."

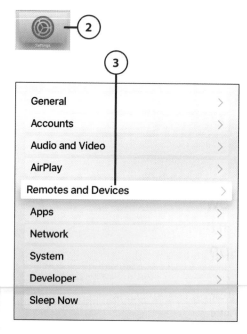

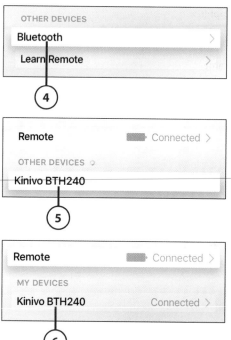

It's Not All Good

Apple TV Doesn't Support Bluetooth Keyboards

If you want to connect a Bluetooth keyboard to your Apple TV to make it easier to type in passwords and searches, there's bad news: The Apple TV doesn't support Bluetooth keyboards (or any kind of keyboards). This is a surprise; previous generations did. Support will possibly be added later, but as of now, there's no way for a keyboard to work with your Apple TV.

How to Connect a Third-Party Game Controller to Apple TV

Every game that runs on the Apple TV can be played using the remote control—but that doesn't mean it should. Some games require a more sophisticated and powerful game controller. If you want to use one of those controllers to play console-style games, follow these steps to connect the controller to the Apple TV:

1. You'll need a controller that supports Bluetooth. Put it into pairing mode (consult the manual or manufacturer if it's not obvious how to do this).

2. On the Apple TV, use the remote to launch Settings.

3. Select Remotes and Devices.

4. Select Bluetooth from the Other Devices menu.

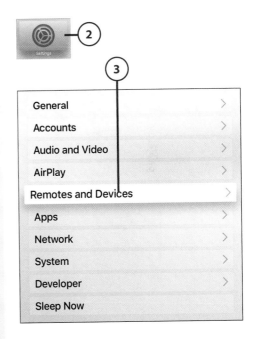

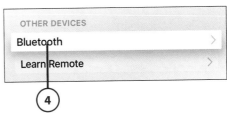

5. Look for the controller in the Other Devices section. Select it.

6. After a few moments, the controller should connect to the Apple TV. You'll see it show up in the My Devices menu, listed as Connected.

Now, whenever you want to play a game, just pick up that controller and you'll be ready to go.

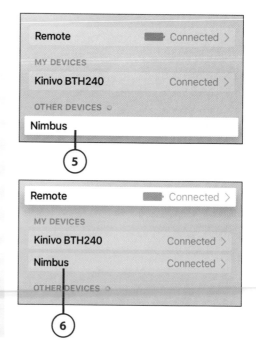

Using the Remote App

As mentioned earlier in the book, the Siri Remote isn't the only remote Apple product that can control the Apple TV. There's also the Remote app. This free app has been around for years—it worked with older versions of the Apple TV, too—and provides most of the features of the Siri Remote, and some it doesn't have.

In order to use the Remote app, you need:

- An iOS device—an iPhone, iPad, or iPod touch

- The Remote app installed on that device (get it at the iOS App Store)

- The iOS device and Apple TV to be on the same Wi-Fi network.

How to Set Up the Remote App

After you've got the app installed on your iOS device, here's what you need to do to configure Remote to control your Apple TV:

1. Tap the Remote app to launch it.

2. Tap Set Up Home Sharing.

3. Enter your Apple ID. (You should be using the same Apple ID on your iOS device and your Apple TV.)

4. Tap Sign In.

5. A confirmation that Home Sharing is enabled on your iOS device appears. Tap OK.

6. On your Apple TV, enable Home Sharing. For instructions on how to do that, check out "Enable Home Sharing" in Chapter 3. (not pictured)

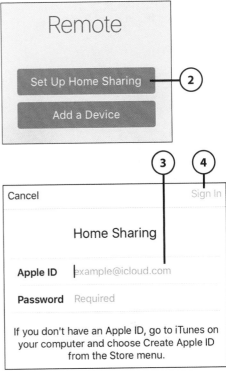

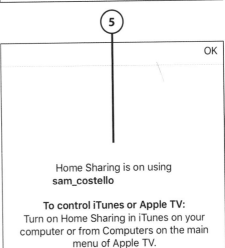

7. With that done, an icon for your Apple TV will appear in the Remote app.

How to Use the Remote App

After you've got Remote set up, it's time to start using it. Here's what you need to know:

1. Tap the Remote app to launch it.

2. Tap the icon for your Apple TV.

3. This is main screen for the Remote app. The middle section of the screen works just like the touchpad on the Siri Remote. Swipe left and right, up and down to navigate the Apple TV. Tap the screen to select items.

4. On screens where you can enter text, a keyboard icon appears in the top left corner (it's hidden if there's no option to enter text). Tap it to bring up the iOS device's onscreen keyboard. This make entering usernames and passwords much easier.

5. To get tips about how to use the Remote app, tap the question mark icon in the top right.

6. The three-line icon on the bottom left of Remote opens onscreen menus, when available. You won't encounter these menus too often on the Apple TV.

7. The Menu button in Remote works exactly like the Menu button on the Siri Remote: Use it to go back, start the screensaver, and more.

8. The play/pause button in Remote performs the same functions as the identical button on the Siri Remote.

It's Not All Good

Remote Doesn't Support Siri or Games

The Remote app can do almost everything the Siri Remote does, with two big exceptions: Siri and games. As of this writing, you can't speak to the Remote app to search for content or perform tasks like launching apps or getting more information about a movie. Only the Siri Remote can do that right now. Apple has promised to add that feature to the app in 2016, though.

The Siri Remote can be used to control every game on the Apple TV. The same isn't true of the Remote app. In fact, in my (somewhat limited) testing, the Remote app couldn't play any games at all.

Using Siri to Control the Apple TV

The coolest feature of the Apple TV might be that you can control almost every aspect of it using your voice. The touchpad works, too, but why swipe and click when you can talk?

The Apple TV uses Siri to listen to and respond to your questions and commands. This is the same Siri that you might have used on the iPhone or iPad, but it's not the same Siri that didn't work so well a few years ago. Unlike the iPhone or iPad version of Siri, this one doesn't speak to you. It just shows text on the screen. Even better, the modern version of Siri is smart, fast, and accurate. You'll be surprised how well the Apple TV responds to your voice, even when there's noise nearby.

Activating Siri

Using Siri on the Apple TV is simple. When you want to use Siri, all you need to do is press the Siri button—the one with the microphone icon—on the remote control, and speak. There's no need to hold the remote near your mouth; it's smart enough to hear you.

Push to activate Siri, then speak.

When you hold down the microphone button, Siri appears on the TV screen in the form of a colored bar. The words you speak then display on the screen, and the Apple TV takes action based on what you said.

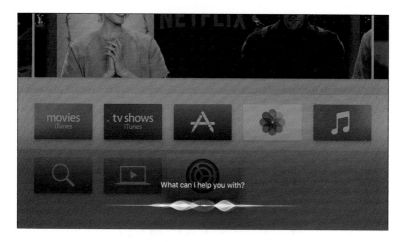

Frequently Used Siri Commands

Siri is so powerful and so good at understanding what we mean when we speak to it. The list of commands and phrases it can respond to is truly impressive. Experiment by talking to Siri and you'll start to learn what works best. In the meantime, here are some common phrases that are sure to work. Just be sure to press the Siri button on the remote before speaking.

"What Did She/He Just Say?"

Did you miss a key bit of dialogue or want to confirm that you heard what you think you did? Say "What did she say?" and three things happen: Your video jumps back 15 seconds, the volume increases for a short time, and closed captioning is briefly turned on.

"Turn On Closed Captioning"

If you, or someone watching with you, requires closed captioning to enjoy a movie or TV show, you don't need to wade through the Settings app. Instead, just say "Turn on closed captioning" and the Apple TV asks what language you want the closed captions in. Select one and text displays onscreen right away.

"Play from the Beginning"

Jump back to the start of a movie or TV episode by telling Siri to "Play from the beginning." Similar phrases like "Start at the beginning" should work, too.

"Fast Forward/Rewind x Minutes"

As we learned earlier in this chapter, you can jump forward and backward in videos by swiping across the touchpad at the top of the remote. You can do the same thing—but even more precisely—using your voice. "Fast forward 3 minutes" jumps you forward exactly three minutes, while "Rewind 2 minutes" takes you back that amount time, no swiping required. Phrases like "skip forward" or "go back" work as well.

"Who Directed This Movie?"

Do you want more detail about the movie or TV show you're watching? Siri can help. Ask "Who directed this movie?" to get a snippet of information about the director. Similar questions such as "Who stars in this movie?" also get you useful details.

When you ask the question, use the remote to select a result to get more information about people involved in the movie. For more about what information you can get about directors, actors, and other professionals, check out "Learn About the Movie You're Watching" in Chapter 3, "Using iTunes for TV and Movies."

"Launch App"

Siri lets you launch any app or game installed on your Apple TV just by saying "Launch [the name of the app]."

Ask Questions

Siri knows the answer to all kinds of questions. The questions are too extensive to list here, of course, but these should give you a sense of the sorts of things you can find out:

- "What time is in it [*city*]?"
- "What is [*company's*] stock price?"
- "Who won the 1980 World Series?"
- "Who are the [*team name*] playing next?"

Speak Famous Movie Quotes

Sometimes, if you speak a famous movie quote, Siri knows what movie the quote comes from and recommends it to you. I used the following quotes, but I'm sure there are others for you to discover:

- "Open the pod bay doors."
- "Play it again, Sam."
- "I'll be back."
- "ET phone home."

"What Is the Temperature?"

If you're planning to head outside after finishing what you're watching, Siri can help you dress appropriately. Just ask, "What is the temperature?" and weather details pop up on the screen without interrupting your movie or TV show.

Are you curious to know what the weather is like elsewhere? Try "What's the weather like in [*another city or county*]?" to find out.

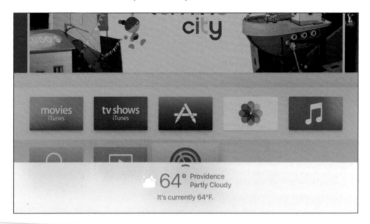

Swipe up to get an hour-by-hour forecast and information such as the chance of rain, the humidity, and what temperature it feels like outside.

>>>*Go Further*

GET THE FULL WEATHER FORECAST

Siri can give you more information about the weather than just what's happening outside your window right now. Ask Siri for the forecast and you'll get the projected weather for up to the next 10 days. Swipe up on the remote, and the tray expands to show more detail about each upcoming day.

"What's the Score?"

Siri can give you sports scores without leaving whatever app you're using. For instance, if you're watching a movie but want to know who's ahead in the Patriots game, just ask "What's the score of the Patriots game?" or "What are the NBA scores?" to get a quick score check.

Swiping up expands the tray at the bottom of the screen to give you full detail about the action, including current scores, how much time is left in each game, and where you can watch the games.

>>>Go Further

SIRI CAN CONTROL MUSIC, TOO

Siri is a champ at controlling the music you listen to on your Apple TV, too. For a full set of music-related commands, check out Chapter 6, "Music Television: Music on the Apple TV." The things you can tell Siri to do are sprinkled throughout that chapter.

Searching the Apple TV

Search is at the heart of what the Apple TV does best. Forget about flipping through the channels trying to find something to watch. With the Apple TV, you can search for virtually anything you want to watch and find it (within reason). You can browse through the apps on your Apple TV, of course, but searching is much cooler.

Universal Search

By far the coolest search feature of the Apple TV is universal search. To understand what it is, think of a search engine. If you search for "Apple TV" at Google, you get all the websites Google thinks are relevant to that phrase. But imagine a search engine that delivers results from Google, Bing, Yahoo!, and DuckDuckGo all in one place. That's what universal search does, except for video content.

On the Apple TV, searching for a movie—for example, Mad Max Fury Road — shows you all the places you can watch it. So, the search results page tells you that you can buy and rent Mad Max Fury Road at iTunes, or stream it at HBO and Netflix. No longer must you search in each app individually; one search gets you everything you need.

All searches for movies and TV on the Apple TV are universal searches; there is no need to specify that you want it.

It's Not All Good

The Limits of Universal Search

Universal search has some limits: It can only search apps you have installed on your device and that support the feature. As of this writing, the only Apple TV apps that support universal search are

- HBO GO/HBO NOW

- Hulu

- iTunes

- Netflix

- PBS/PBS Kids

- Showtime

Other apps will be added over time, making the search even more universal. Many more might be available by the time you read this, but for now be aware that these are the only compatible apps.

How to Search Using Siri

When you're looking for something to watch, you'll find it much faster by searching for it. The search features on the Apple TV are so smart that you won't have to search by name—you can search broad categories or vague topics and then have the Apple TV refine the results until you find just what you want.

To find content by searching, follow these steps:

1. Press the Siri button on the remote.

2. Search for something. You'll have the best luck if you start your searches with clear commands such as "Show me" or "Find me." For example, "Show me horror movies from the 1980s" or "Find me TV shows starring Gillian Anderson."

Searching for Exactly What You Want Is a Snap

It should come as no surprise that searching for exactly what you want is easy on the Apple TV. Looking for Mad Men season 7? Just say "Show me Mad Men season 7" and the show will appear in no time.

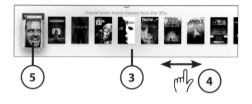

3. The Apple TV displays results matching your search in a bar along the bottom of the screen.

4. Use the touchpad on the remote to swipe side to side across the results.

5. To view more information about an individual result, click the touchpad to make the selection. For more detail about what you see when you do this, check out "Anatomy of the Search Results Screen" later in this chapter.

You don't have to be content with your first set of search results. Siri makes refining your searches as you go easy.

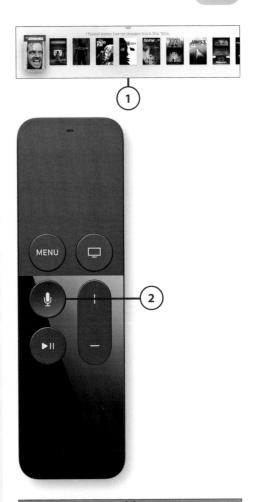

Refine Your Searches

After you have a basic set of search results, Siri can help you narrow them down by making them more specific. To do that:

1. Make sure you've run a search already.

2. Press the Siri button on the remote.

3. Say the criteria you want to use to improve your search. For instance, if your original search was for horror movies of the 1980s, you could refine it by saying "just ones directed by Wes Craven" or "only ones rated PG-13." Using words like "just" or "only" helps Siri narrow your results.

4. Siri updates the results in the tray along the bottom of the screen to match the new criteria you used to narrow the search.

When you're refining your search results, use information such as actors, directors, years, star rating, age ratings, and genre to get more specific.

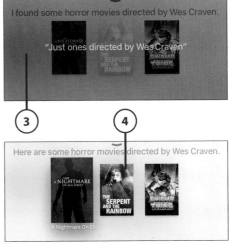

>>>*Go Further*

TRY A VAGUE SEARCH USING SIRI

Let's say you know that one of your favorite actors guest starred on a show, but you don't know what season or what episode it was. Siri can help. Just ask Siri to show you that episode. For instance, if you want to see the episode of *Weeds* that guest starred Snoop Dogg (and who wouldn't?), ask Siri to "Show me the episode of *Weeds* starring Snoop Dogg" and the episode will be onscreen in no time. Of course, you might still need to rent or buy it if you don't subscribe to a service that has it for free, but at least you know where to find it.

Search Using the Search App

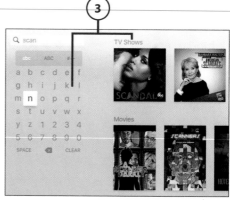

Siri isn't the only way to search for things on your Apple TV. A built-in app, Search, is dedicated to searching. It can search both the content of your Apple TV and apps that offer web-based content, such as iTunes, Netflix, and HBO. To use Search to find what you're looking for, do the following:

1. Launch the Search app from the home screen.

2. Use the onscreen keyboard or the Remote app to enter a search term.

3. As you type, search results begin to automatically populate the screen. When you see what you're looking for, use the remote to highlight and select it.

Anatomy of the Search Results Screen

After you find something you're interested in, select it with the remote's touchpad and then click the touchpad to see more about that item. When you do that, the screen offers the following information:

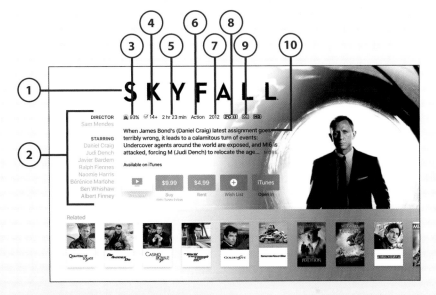

1. **Title**—The title of the movie or TV show.

2. **Director and Stars**—The names of the director and stars of the movie or TV show appear along the side of the screen.

3. **Rotten Tomatoes Rating**—The item's rating from Rotten Tomatoes, a website that combines critics' and ordinary users' reviews. A 100 is a perfect score.

4. **Common Sense Rating**—The suggested minimum age that the movie or TV show is appropriate for.

5. **Length**—The item's running time.

6. **Genre**—The genre to which the movie or TV show belongs.

7. **Year**—The year the item was released.

8. **MPAA Rating**—The rating assigned to a movie by the Motion Picture Association: PG, R, and so on.

9. **Closed Captioning**—Indicates that the program is available with Closed Captioning for the hearing impaired.

10. **Synopsis**—A short description of what the movie or TV show is about.

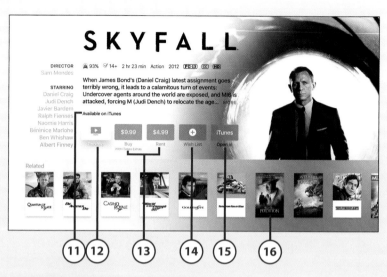

11. **Available On**—This is a feature of the Apple TV's universal search, showing you which services offer the item. Use the remote to highlight different apps to see pricing and other options for that service.

12. **Preview**—Watch the trailer for the movie by selecting this button.

13. **Buy/Rent**—Choose how you want to enjoy the item (if the item is available free in one of your apps, this button is not shown when that app is selected).

14. **Wish List**—Save the item to watch later by selecting this.

15. **Open In**—Jump to the app selected in Available On, where you can see information about the program.

16. **Related**—If you're curious to check out other content that's related to this, select something from the Related row at the bottom of the screen.

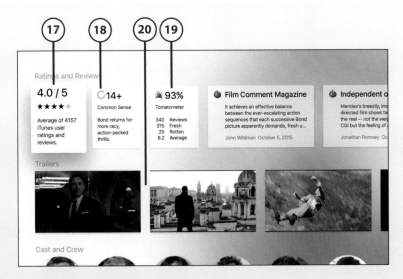

17. **iTunes User Reviews**—The average review given to the movie by all iTunes users who have rated it.

18. **Common Sense Media Rating**—More detail behind the Common Sense rating shown earlier. This provides more context to help parents decide whether it's appropriate.

19. **Rotten Tomatoes details**—More information about the Rotten Tomatoes ratings for the film, including excerpts from reviews of the item (swipe left and right across the review to read more).

20. **Trailers**—The theatrical previews for the film, included to give you more teasers.

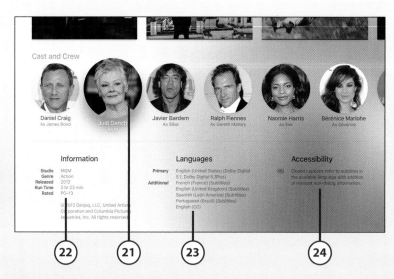

21. **Cast and Crew**—Browse the cast and crew from the movie using the touchpad. To learn more about a person, click the touchpad.

22. **Movie information**—Some basic details about the movie, such as the studio that produced it, its genre, the year it was released, its length, and its MPAA rating.

23. **Languages**—The list of all languages the movie is available in, both in spoken language and in subtitles.

24. **Accessibility**—Information about the accessibility features of the film, such as closed captions.

If you decide you're not interested in this item, click the Menu button on the remote to get back to your search results or speak a new search to Siri.

>>>Go Further
SEARCH WITHIN APPS

Search on the Apple TV isn't just for finding movies and TV shows to watch using universal search. You can also search for content within apps that support search. To do that, look for a search menu in those apps (for instance, check out the search tutorials for apps such as Netflix, Hulu, and HBO GO/NOW in Chapter 4, "Using Other Video Apps: Netflix, HBO, and More"). You'll probably have to type in your searches; most apps don't support Siri for searching themselves yet.

iTunes offers a host of movies and TV shows available for subscription (TV shows), rental (movies), and purchase (both).

The first two apps on your Apple TV home screen let you access iTunes' huge collection of movies and TV shows. With it, you'll never be wanting for something to watch. In this chapter, you'll learn about:

→ Renting and buying movies at iTunes
→ Buying TV shows at iTunes
→ Using home sharing to watch movies and TV

Using iTunes for TV and Movies

There's a tremendous amount to watch at iTunes, but the Apple TV goes far beyond that. When you're done with this chapter, the next one shows you how to use Netflix, Hulu, HBO, and other video apps.

Renting and Buying Movies at iTunes

The Apple TV makes it easy to rent or buy movies from iTunes and enjoy them on your TV. Just a few commands to Siri or a few clicks on the remote and you'll be watching the latest hits and all-time classics.

Search for Movies

The best and most powerful way to search the Apple TV is to ask Siri to find movies that match what you're interested in. If you would rather not talk to your TV, though, traditional searches still work.

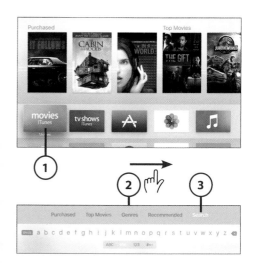

1. Start at the home screen of the Apple TV and launch the iTunes Movies app.

2. Swipe across the touchpad to move along the menus at the top of the screen until you've highlighted Search.

3. Click the touchpad to choose Search.

4. Use the onscreen keyboard to type in the name of the movie, actor, or director you're looking for. You can also hold down the Siri button and speak your search. Items matching your search appear at the bottom of the screen.

Go Faster with the Remote App

Talking to Siri is the fastest way to search the Apple TV for movies and TV shows, but another quick option is the Remote app. This app—free from Apple—runs on the iPhone, iPod touch, and iPad. Among other features, it lets you type using your device's onscreen keyboard. Get it at the iOS App Store.

5. When you've found a movie that looks interesting, use the touchpad to highlight it and then click the touchpad to learn more about it.

For an explanation of the options included on the screen about the movie you've selected, check out "Anatomy of the Movie Detail Screen" later in this chapter.

Browsing Movies

If you don't have a clear idea of what you feel like watching, or would like to discover movies that pique your interest based on their names or posters, try browsing the iTunes Movies app. There are two options for browsing: by featured releases and by genre.

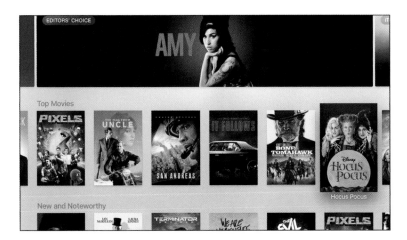

Browse Featured Releases

Featured releases are the movies that Apple promotes on the main screen of the iTunes Movies app. They might be new releases, classics notable because of recent events, themed collections, and movies that are on sale.

When you launch the iTunes Movies app, you're delivered directly to the main featured releases screen. Navigate it using the touchpad and click to select individual movies or collections that contain multiple movies.

Browse By Genre

Browsing by genre lets you dive deep into a specific type of movie, such as Action, Documentary, or Romance, and see what's available. To browse by genre:

1. Launch the iTunes Movies app.

2. Swipe across the touchpad to move the selector along the menus at the top of the screen until you reach Genres.

3. Click the touchpad to choose Genres.

4. The list of available genres appears on the right side of the screen. Use the remote to move through the list, and click the touchpad when you find a genre you're interested in to see what's available.

5. The next screen is the featured releases for the genre you choose. It includes a series of promoted items along the top (swipe side to side across them to see more), popular items, and then a few rows of additional options. Use the touchpad to move up and down and left and right through the available movies.

6. When you find a movie you're interested in, highlight it using the touchpad and click the touch-pad to make your selection.

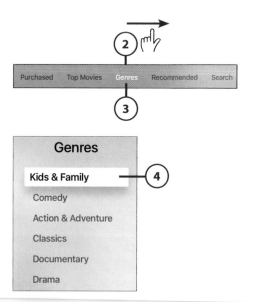

Anatomy of the Movie Detail Screen

When you select a movie that you're interested in, the screen that displays its details looks almost identical to what we saw in Chapter 2, "Controlling Your Apple TV: The Remote, Siri, and Search," in the "Anatomy of the Search Results Screen" section. For a full discussion of the options and features there, check out the previous chapter.

In this case, the major difference is that this isn't a universal search; the information displayed on this screen is specific to just the iTunes Movies app.

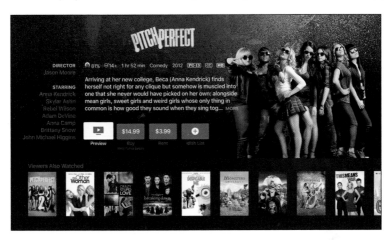

Rent and Buy Movies

After you find a movie you want to watch, you can either rent or buy it. Renting it lets you watch it once, whereas buying the movie costs more, but it becomes part of your personal library forever and you can watch it as many times as you like.

When you're on the movie detail screen, follow these steps to rent or buy a movie:

1. Use the remote to highlight and select the Rent or Buy button, whichever you prefer.

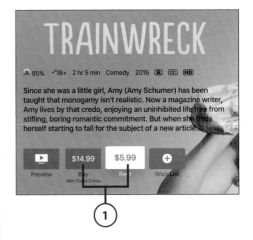

2. Your options are to rent/buy the movie and watch it right away, watch it later, or cancel. Make your selection using the remote.

3. Because all purchases on the Apple TV are billed through the card on file in your Apple ID, you need to sign in to that account using your password.

4. With that, the movie is purchased or rented, and ready. On the movie detail screen, the play button is activated. You'll also find the movie in other places in the iTunes Movies app, as discussed in the "Watch Movies" section of this chapter.

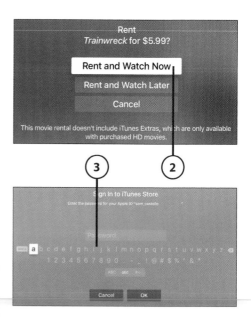

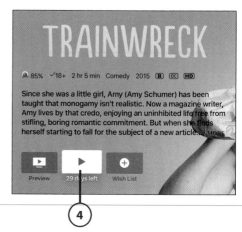

It's Not All Good

Some Movies Can't Be Rented

Every movie in the iTunes Movies app can be purchased, but not every one can be rented. The movie studios that release movies to iTunes determine how they're offered: purchase only or purchase and rental. Older movies are generally available both ways, whereas some new releases can only be purchased initially and then become available to rent weeks or months later.

Rules for Rentals

When you rent a movie from iTunes, you need to know these rules:

- The rental is good for 30 days. If you don't watch it within 30 days, it expires and you're out whatever you paid for it—no refunds.

- After you start watching a rental, you have 24 hours to finish it (in the United States; it's 48 hours in some other countries). You can pause the movie and come back to it later, but if you come back more than 24 hours later, the rental will have expired without you finishing the movie and, again, you can't get your money back.

- You can watch a movie as many times as you want in the 24-hour rental period.

>>>Go Further

PRE-ORDERING MOVIES

Is there a movie you love so much you can't wait to own it? For some movies, you don't have to wait until the day they're released to buy them. You can pre-order them.

Pre-ordering lets you buy a movie now and have it automatically added to your iTunes movie library when it's released.

Movies that you can pre-order show up in the iTunes Movies app like any other movie, but when you go to their detail page, you'll see a pre-order button instead of rent or buy.

Watch Movies

If you chose not to watch your movie right away when you rented or bought it, you can find and watch it by following these steps:

1. If you have the iTunes Movies app in your first row of icons, highlight that app and the movie should appear in the row at the very top of the screen. Select it and skip to step 6 of this tutorial.

2. If the movie doesn't appear in the row at the top of the screen, you may have rented or bought other movies that are displayed instead of the movie you're looking for. Launch the iTunes Movies app.

3. In the row of options at the top of the screen, highlight Purchased and select it by clicking the touchpad.

4. In the menu at the left side of the screen, select Rentals (or another category that the movie would be in, such as Recent or its genre).

5. When you select a category in the left-hand menu, the movies in that category appear on the right. Use the remote to navigate to the movie you want to watch and select it.

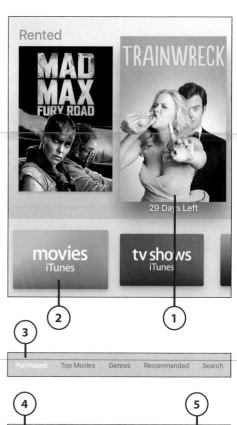

6. On the movie detail screen, highlight the play button and click the touchpad on the remote to start the movie.

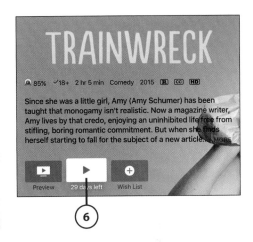

>>>Go Further

HEAR THE DIALOGUE WITH REDUCE LOUD SOUNDS

Have you noticed that some movies have a weird balance of the volume levels for music, sound effects, and dialogue? You get super-loud sound effects and music, but can't hear the dialogue without turning the sound up so loud that you practically go deaf when a noisy effect occurs.

Instead of fighting an endless losing battle with your volume buttons, you can use an Apple TV feature called Reduce Loud Sounds, which automatically balances the volume level of dialogue and sound effects for an easier-on-the-ears experience.

Enable Reduce Loud Sounds by pressing the Siri button on the remote and saying, "Turn on Reduce Loud Sounds."

Learn About the Movie You're Watching

If you get curious about the actors, director, or background of the movie you're watching, Siri can help. You can ask a number of questions, but here's one good example to give you an idea of what's possible.

1. Press the Siri button on the remote.

2. When the Siri prompt appears on the screen say, "Who stars in this movie?" (not pictured).

3. A tray slides up from the bottom of the screen showing the photos and names of the actors with major roles in the movie. Because this is shown in a small tray at the bottom of the screen, your movie continues to play.

4. You can use the remote to move across each actor's photo. Click the trackpad to get more information about the actor you've highlighted.

5. The movie automatically pauses and is replaced with information about the actor you chose, including his or her name and headshot, as well as some basic information about the actor from Wikipedia (click the Wikipedia link to read more). Below that are selections of movies and TV shows the actor appears in. Select them to see more about those programs.

6. To return to the movie you were watching, press the Menu button on the remote. When you get back to the movie, it automatically starts playing again.

Other Searches

You can get this same kind of information about directors by asking Siri "Who directed this?" As always, you can ask all the types of questions covered in Chapter 2's "Frequently Used Siri Commands."

Watch Previous iTunes Movie Purchases

If you're already an Apple user, you might have purchased movies from iTunes on your computer or iOS device. If so, you can watch all of your purchased movies on your Apple TV. Here's how:

1. On the home screen of the Apple TV, select the iTunes Movies app.

2. In the app, use the touchpad to navigate the menus at the top of the screen and select Purchased.

3. Use the left-hand menu to locate and select a category that contains the movies you're looking for.

4. Use the remote to highlight and select one of the movies on the right side of the screen.

5. The movie's detail screen appears, where you can watch the trailer (click the Preview button) or play the movie.

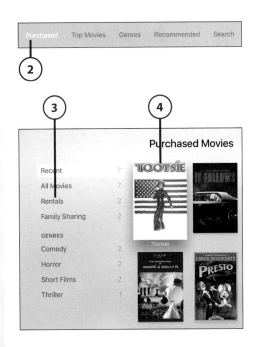

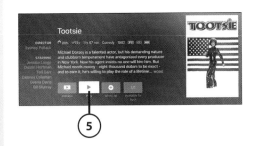

Turn on Subtitles for Movies and TV

The Apple TV makes it pretty easy to watch a movie or TV show with the subtitles turned on. Just follow these steps:

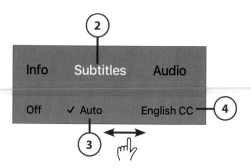

1. With a movie or TV show already playing, swipe down on the touchpad on the remote to reveal a tray at the top of the screen.

2. Use the touchpad to highlight and select the Subtitles menu.

3. Browse through the available sub-title languages using the touch-pad.

4. When you find the language you want, click the touchpad to start displaying the subtitles.

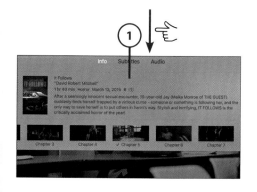

Turn Subtitles Off

To turn off subtitles, follow the pre-ceding steps but select Off in step 4. Subtitles aren't available for all movies and TV shows—it's up to the people who produced the program to include them—but they're present for many things.

>>>Go Further
TURN SUBTITLES ON AND OFF WITH SIRI

The easier way to turn subtitles on and off is Siri. Just tell Siri, "Turn on subtitles" and you'll get subtitles right away. Turn them off again by saying, "Turn off sub-titles." Pretty simple!

Buying TV Shows at iTunes

We live in the New Golden Age of TV, so there's a good chance that you'll watch a lot more TV shows on your Apple TV than movies. If so, iTunes is a great place to get both the latest episodes and to catch up on earlier seasons of your favorite shows.

Search for TV Shows

Like with movies, you can use Siri to search for TV shows by voice and get results via universal search. Searches such as, "Show me TV shows starring Julianna Margulies" or "Find me the episode of Homicide with Jake Gyllenhaal" will get you what you want very quickly.

A more traditional search is also an option. Just follow these steps:

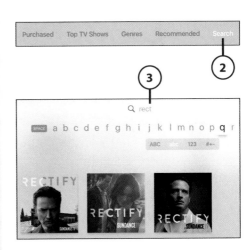

1. On the Apple TV home screen, select the iTunes TV Shows app.

2. Use the touchpad to move the selector across the menu at the top of the screen and select Search.

3. Type in what you're looking for using the onscreen keyboard or the Remote app. A set of results appears below the search bar. Series aren't represented by a single result. Instead, each season of a given series shows up as a separate result.

4. When you find a show you're interested in, click the touchpad to select it.

Search Using Siri

Remember: The Apple TV's universal search can look for TV shows, too. If you want to find a series or episode, you can search using Siri, not just these instructions.

5. On the season detail page, you can get information about that season, its episodes, and how to watch it.

It's Not All Good

You Can't Rent TV Shows

Renting movies is an affordable and fun way to check out a flick, but there's no equivalent for TV shows. You buy them or you don't watch them (from iTunes, at least). Apple's logic for this is that individual TV episodes are so cheap—usually around $3 an episode—that people would rather just own them. I suspect that Apple might just not want to deal with the overhead of supporting TV show rentals, but either way, if you want TV episodes from iTunes, you're buying them.

Browse TV Shows

Just like with movies, the fastest way to find what you're looking for on Apple TV is to search. But if you're not sure what you're in the mood for and prefer to browse, that option is available, too. To browse the available TV shows:

1. Launch the iTunes TV Shows app.

2. The default screen shown to you is Top TV Shows. Other options in the menu at the top of the screen are Genres and Recommended.

3. On the Top TV Shows screen, you can use the remote control to move up and down through the shows.

4. If you select the Genres menu at the top of the screen, a list of genres appears on the right side of the screen. Swipe up and down on the genres and click the touchpad to select one you're interested in.

5. The home screen of the genre you chose displays a set of featured items across the top, Top TV Shows in the genre beneath that, and then other recent and popular series. Use the remote to navigate up and down, and left and right on this screen.

6. The Recommended screen provides TV shows you might be interested in based on other TV shows you've bought from iTunes.

7. For all three screens, when you've found something you're interested in, highlight it and click the touchpad to select the option.

8. The detail page appears, which lists information about that season, its episodes, and how to watch them.

Don't Buy TV at iTunes Without a Search

Before you spend money at iTunes on a TV show, make sure you perform a search with Siri. Because Siri's universal search checks multiple apps for what you're looking for, you might discover that the show you want is also available at Netflix or Hulu. If you subscribe to those services, you'll be able to watch the show there for no additional money, whereas you have to pay separately at iTunes. A search can save you some money.

Buy TV Shows

After you find a TV show you want to watch, it's time to buy. Just follow these steps:

1. Use the remote to highlight and select the Buy button for either an individual episode or the full season, depending on what you want.

2. This screen clearly lists what you're buying and how much it costs. If you've changed your mind, select Cancel. To continue, select Buy.

3. As with any purchase, you need to authorize the use of your Apple ID. Do so by typing in your Apple ID password using the onscreen keyboard or Remote app. Select OK to continue.

4. You've now purchased the episode or season. The detail screen reappears, where you can start watching your purchase.

Buy a Season Pass

Besides buying a single episode of TV or an entire season, you can also buy a Season Pass. A Season Pass is a pre-order for the entire current season of a show. You don't buy Season Passes for older shows—you just buy their entire seasons in a single purchase—but you can get one for shows that are currently airing.

If you buy a Season Pass, each time a new episode is released (usually the day after it airs on TV), it becomes available to you via iTunes. Season Passes often cost slightly less than buying each episode individually.

To buy a Season Pass, begin by finding the series whose current season you want to buy using the techniques already discussed in this chapter. Select the series to get to the detail page, and then:

1. Highlight and select the Buy Season Pass button.

2. A screen appears that explains what you're buying and for how much. Select Cancel if you've changed your mind. Select Buy to continue.

3. Enter your Apple ID password and tap OK to finalize the purchase.

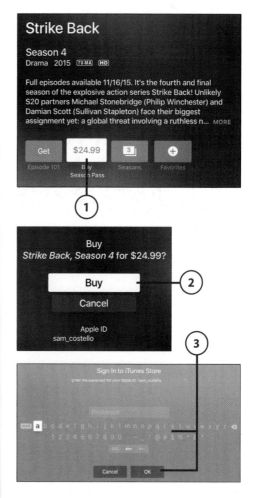

Get New Episodes Via Season Pass

One of the benefits of buying a Season Pass is that you don't have to go hunting for each new episode of a series as it's released. Instead, the episodes come right to you. To find them:

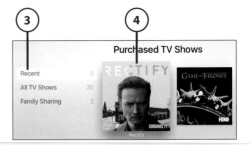

1. Launch the iTunes TV Shows app.

2. Select the Purchased menu at the top of the screen.

3. In the menu on the left, select the category that contains the show (Recent or All TV Shows).

4. The shows contained in the category you selected appear at the right. Use the remote to navigate to the show whose episode you want to watch. Click the touchpad to select that show.

5. All the episodes of the season you've bought appear here. Swipe left to right to navigate through the episodes. The newest episode is at the far right of the list. Click the touchpad to play it.

Watch TV Shows

When you're watching TV episodes on the Apple TV, you have the following options for controlling the playback:

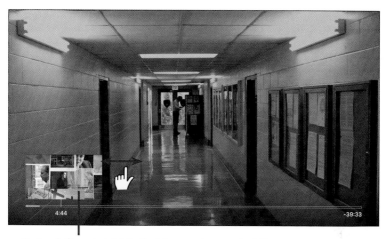

Swipe left and right to fast forward or rewind the current program

Fast Forward and Reverse. As with movies, swiping left to right takes you forward, while swiping right to left goes back. The faster you swipe, the faster you move through the program. Click the touchpad to jump to a new location.

Swipe down to access information about a show

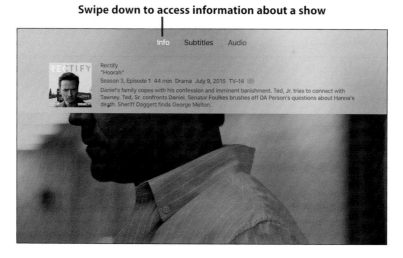

Get Information. To get information about the episode you're watching, swipe down on the touchpad and highlight the Info tab.

Swipe down to access subtitle controls

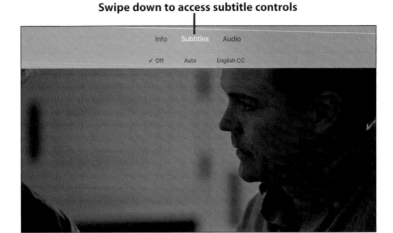

| Info | Subtitles | Audio |

| ✓ Off | Auto | English CC |

Turn On Subtitles. As already covered in this chapter, you can turn subtitles on and off, when they're available, by swiping down on the touchpad.

Swipe down to access audio options

| Info | Subtitles | Audio |

LANGUAGE	SOUND	SPEAKERS
✓ English (United States)	✓ Full Dynamic Range	✓ Apple TV
	Reduce Loud Sounds	◀) bedroom
		◀) kitchen

Change Audio Options. To change the audio options, swipe down on the touchpad and select the Audio menu. In it, your options include choosing the language for the program, using standard sound or reducing loud sounds to make it easier to hear dialogue, or send the audio to a set of speakers other than the ones attached to the TV.

Learn More About What You're Watching

You can learn more about the TV shows by asking Siri about them, just like you can with movies. Check out "Learn About the Movie You're Watching" earlier in this chapter for examples of the kinds of information Siri can deliver.

Watch Previous iTunes TV Show Purchases

If you've previously purchased TV episodes or seasons at iTunes to watch on your computer, iOS device, or even an earlier model of the Apple TV, you can watch them on your television. Here's how:

1. On the home screen of the Apple TV, select the iTunes TV Shows app.

2. Scroll to and select the Purchased option at the top of the screen. A menu appears on the left side of the screen that lists Recent purchases, All TV Shows you've bought, and shows available via Family Sharing (if there are any and you have Family Sharing enabled).

3. Use the remote to highlight the menu you want to look at. When you do this, the right side of the screen updates to show the content in that menu.

4. Highlight and select the show you want to watch.

5. Navigate to and select the episode you want to watch.

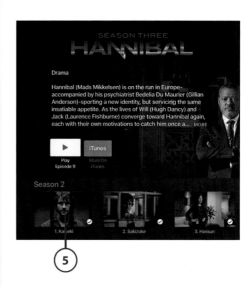

Family Sharing

Family Sharing allows all members of a family to share each other's iTunes and App Store purchases without having to pay for them more than once. To learn how to set up and use Family Sharing, check out http://ipod.about.com/od/FamilySharing/ss/How-to-Set-Up-Family-Sharing-for-iPhone-and-iTunes.htm.

Using Home Sharing to Watch Movies and TV Shows from Your Computer

iTunes is great, but it's far from the only place to get TV shows and movies. Your computer's hard drive might be stuffed full of programs you've gotten from other online stores or by ripping DVDs. If that's the case, don't worry; you can watch that content on the Apple TV, too.

It's Not All Good

Some Media Isn't Apple TV Compatible

Although it's true that most media you get from other stores or from DVDs works on the Apple TV, not all of it does. Some media might have copy protections or be saved in a file format that's not compatible with the Apple TV. You'll have to experiment to see whether any of your existing media library is blocked in that way.

Home Sharing is an Apple technology that allows you to take content stored on your computer's hard drive and use it on your Apple TV—to share it in your home, in other words. It works when both your Mac (or PC running iTunes) and Apple TV are on the same Wi-Fi or Ethernet network, are running iTunes 10.5 or higher, and both have Home Sharing turned on.

It's a great way to get movies, TV shows, music, and other media that you purchased from a company other than Apple onto your Apple TV. To use Home Sharing, you need both your computer (with iTunes running) and Apple TV connected to the same home network.

Enable Home Sharing

To connect your computer and Apple TV using Home Sharing:

1. On your computer, launch iTunes.

2. Tap the File menu.

3. Select Home Sharing.

4. Select Turn On Home Sharing.

5. Click Turn On Home Sharing.

6. Enter your Apple ID and password.

7. Click Turn On Home Sharing.

8. On your Apple TV, select the Computers app on the home screen.

9. In the screen that appears, you can choose to use the Apple ID already in use on your Apple TV, or a new one. Use the Apple ID in use on the computer you're trying to connect to.

10. If you select Use This Apple ID, you'll go to the sign-in screen, where your username is already entered. Select Continue to proceed.

11. Enter your Apple ID password and select Continue.

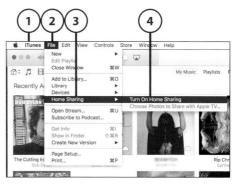

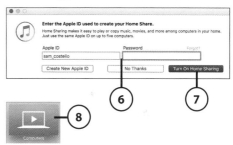

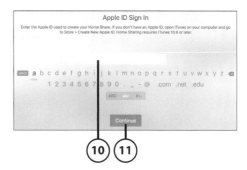

12. With that, Home Sharing is turned on, both devices can connect to each other, and you're ready for the next step.

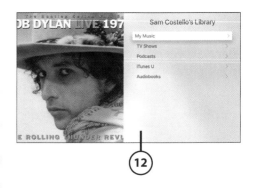

Leave iTunes Open for Home Sharing

For Home Sharing to work, you must leave iTunes running on your computer. If you turn iTunes off, the Apple TV can't connect to your computer or let you access its content.

Watch Movies and TV Shows Using Home Sharing

After you've connected your computer and Apple TV using Home Sharing, it's time to start enjoying content from your computer on your television. (This section focuses on movies and TV shows. Check out Chapter 6, "Music Television: Music on the Apple TV," for Home Sharing of music and Chapter 7, "Advanced TV Topics," for photos.) If that content is movies or TV, here's what you need to do:

1. Launch the Computers app.

2. This menu lists all the categories of content stored on your computer that can be accessed using Home Sharing. What you see here depends on what content you have and what Home Sharing settings you've chosen during set up. Select a menu.

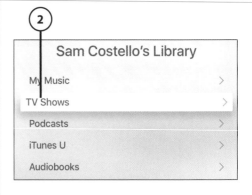

3. Sort the content using the buttons at the top. For TV shows, those buttons are Unwatched, By Show, or By Date. Select the option you prefer.

4. Select the episode you want to watch and it begins playing.

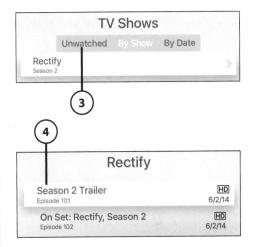

Downloading apps, like Netflix, from the App Store gives
access to a variety of streaming video providers.

From Netflix to HBO to Hulu and beyond, video apps on the Apple TV provide a virtually unlimited library of content. In this chapter, you'll learn about:

→ Using Network TV apps

→ Using Netflix

→ Using HBO

→ Using Showtime

→ Using Hulu

→ Video apps to check out

Using Other Video Apps: Netflix, HBO, and More

If you've thought about "cutting the cord"—cancelling your cable TV and replacing it with subscriptions to web-based streaming video services—this chapter can help you learn how it works, save money, and transform the way you enjoy movies and TV in your home and on the go.

Using Network TV Apps

One big attraction of the Apple TV is that it puts the power in the hands of the viewer: You can watch your favorite TV shows when you have time, and you're never at the mercy of whatever show a network prefers to broadcast. That's because the apps that TV networks offer for the Apple TV let you watch shows on demand.

Different network apps have different policies—some make every episode of every show available, and some limit you to the most recent 5 or 6 episodes of the current season—but they all give you a new way to get your TV. Also, when you sign into your cable account to use them, most of them are completely free.

Although no TV network apps come pre-installed on the Apple TV, dozens are available in the App Store from major broadcast networks such as ABC and CBS, big-name cable channels like ESPN and FX, and niche channels such as HGTV and Lifetime.

It's Not All Good

Don't Forget Your Cable Subscription

With so many network apps available, it's easy to start dreaming about cutting the cord and just using the apps. Unfortunately, many TV apps require that you have an active cable subscription that includes their channels for you to use them. Unless you sign in to your cable account, some of these apps offer a very small amount of free content; some offer none. For instance, if you don't have a cable plan with IFC or Disney Channel, you won't be able to log in to those apps on the Apple TV. Most TV apps are another way to see content you already have access to, not a way to get new things for free.

For more about this, check out "It's Not All Good: Sometimes You Need Cable" in Chapter 1, "Introduction to Your Apple TV." Some network apps that don't require cable subscriptions are listed later in this chapter.

Watch Network TV Apps

Because you need an active cable or satellite subscription to unlock the full libraries of most network TV apps, you have to sign in to these apps. Each app has a slightly different process for signing in, so these instructions will vary depending on the app you're using. The concept should be the same for each app, though, so look for similar options and you should be fine.

1. Launch the app you want to use (you will have needed to download it from the App Store, of course).

Downloading Apps

For instructions on how to download apps for the Apple TV, including TV network apps, check out "Downloading and Managing Apps" in Chapter 5, "Using Apps and Games."

2. In the app, look for a menu such as "Settings," "Sign In," or "Log In." Use the touchpad to select that menu.

3. Different apps work in different ways, but generally speaking, the app gives you a web address you need to go to so you can enter a code that activates the app and signs you in to your account. The Apple TV doesn't have a web browser, so you'll need to use your computer or mobile device.

4. When you go to that web address, enter the activation code displayed on the Apple TV.

5. Click Submit.

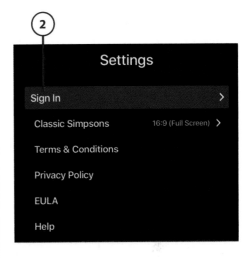

6. Select your cable or satellite provider. This is the company from which you get your TV. Depending on the app you're using, the list of companies to choose from might be relatively short or might include dozens of companies. When you find your cable company, select it. (Depending on the app, this step might come slightly earlier in the process.)

7. Next, log in to your cable or satellite account. This isn't your Apple ID, your Wi-Fi password, or any other account. Rather, this is the username and password you use when you go to your cable company's website and sign in to your account to pay bills, get support, or change your service. If you're not sure what your username and password are for this account, contact your provider.

8. When you're successfully signed in, the Apple TV updates to indicate that your activation was successful.

9. Press the Menu button to go back and start using the app.

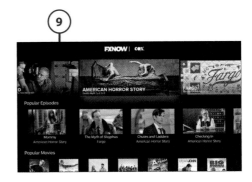

Network TV Apps with Streaming Services

Even though most TV apps block you from using them unless you already subscribe to them on cable, a few networks offer their own streaming servic-es in which you pay a flat monthly fee for access to their shows on your Apple TV. With these services, you can stream whatever's available without needing cable at all. Networks with this kind of service include:

- **CBS All Access**—$6/month

- **HBO Now**— $15/month

- **Lifetime Movie Club**—$4/month

- **Nickelodeon Noggin**—$6/month

- **Seeso**—$4/month for NBC-centric comedies

- **Showtime**—$11/month

- **WWE Network**—$10/month

Not all of these services are available on the Apple TV yet, and some like Seeso haven't launched yet, but they should arrive sooner than later.

It's Not All Good

No Amazon Prime Video—For Now

The Apple TV has apps for most of the major video streaming services: iTunes, Netflix, Hulu, HBO, Showtime, and more. But there's one conspicuous absence: Amazon Prime Video. As of this writing, there is no Prime Video app for the Apple TV. As this book was printed, new reports indicated that a Prime Video app was coming soon. By the time you read this, the app might already be available.

Using Netflix

Almost everyone knows Netflix and how, for less than the price of a movie ticket each month, it gives you access to tens of thousands of movies and TV shows over the Internet. The Apple TV and Netflix are a match made in heaven—a great service combined with a powerful, easy-to-use device that delivers programming right to your big-screen TV. If you subscribe to Netflix already, you're going to love using it with your Apple TV. If you don't, you might find yourself signing up.

Log In to Your Netflix Account

If you already have a Netflix subscription, you can sign in to your account on the Apple TV and access all of your information—queue, personalized recommendations, recently watched list, and so on—without needing to change your subscription. To do this:

1. Launch the Netflix app.

2. Highlight the Sign In button and click the touchpad.

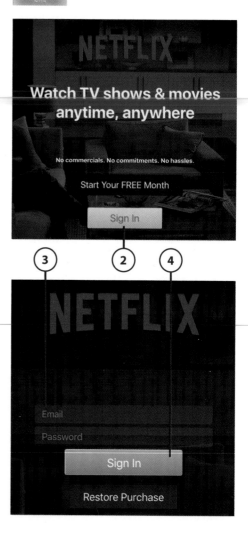

Don't Forget the Remote App

Remember, if you have Apple's free Remote app installed on your iPhone or iPad, you can type using the app's onscreen keyboard. That's much faster and less frustrating than the one-letter-at-a-time option the Apple TV offers.

3. Enter your Netflix username and password.

4. Click the Sign In button.

After you sign in, your Netflix account, queue, and recommendations appear on the screen.

Subscribe to Netflix

If you aren't already a Netflix user, you can become one right from the Apple TV. Just follow these steps:

1. Launch the Netflix app.

2. Highlight the Start Your Free Month button and click the touchpad.

3. Create an account by entering the email address you want to use with this account and creating a password.

4. Highlight Next and click the touchpad.

Email Confirmation
Keep an eye out for confirmation emails to the address you used for your username in step 3.

5. Select what kind of plan you want after your free month ends (assuming you don't cancel, that is). Highlight your choice and click the touchpad.

6. Agree to the terms of service by highlighting Agree and clicking the touchpad.

7. Sign in to your Apple ID account by entering your Apple ID password. This is required because your monthly Netflix subscription is billed to the credit card on file in your Apple ID. Select OK to continue.

8. The next screen makes sure that you understand what you're buying. If you do and want to keep going, highlight Continue and click the touchpad (you can also choose Cancel).

9. Your last chance cancel appears on the confirmation screen. To subscribe, highlight OK and click the touchpad. You're now subscribed to Netflix. The main Netflix screen appears, where you can start finding movies and TV shows to enjoy.

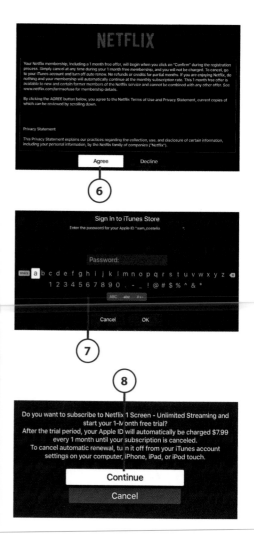

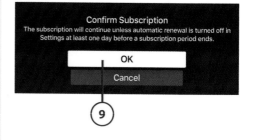

>>>Go Further

USE NETFLIX EVERYWHERE

You might have signed up for Netflix on the Apple TV, but that's not the only place you can use it. In fact, as long as your subscription is paid, you can use it everywhere Netflix works: computers, iPhones and iPads, PlayStation and Xbox, and beyond.

With your subscription, you have unlimited access to stream Netflix movies and TV shows until you cancel. Your subscription is billed each month to the credit card you have on file in your Apple ID. For instructions on how to manage your subscription—including how to cancel it— check out "Managing In-App Purchases and Subscriptions" in Chapter 5.

Search for Movies and TV

The home screen of the Netflix app is packed full of movies and TV shows. Some are items Netflix wants to promote, some are drawn from your list of saved items, and others are grouped by genre and recommended to you by Netflix. Using the Apple TV's remote to navigate this screen and select content is easy. But if you don't see what you want here, you can also search.

1. From the main Netflix screen, swipe up on the touchpad to reveal the Search function.

2. Highlight the Search icon and click the touchpad.

3. Use the onscreen keyboard or the Remote app to search for movies and TV shows by name, director, actor, and other criteria. As you type, search results appear beneath the keyboard. Use the remote to navigate through the results.

4. Highlight a result and click the touchpad to see more information about it.

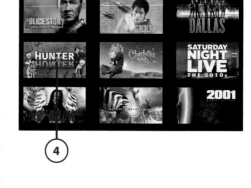

④

Don't Forget Universal Search

Remember: The Apple TV's universal search feature includes Netflix, so if you use Siri to search for movies and TV, you'll get results from Netflix as well as other major apps.

Add Movies and TV Shows to Your Netflix Queue

Your queue is the list of movies and TV shows you've saved to watch later. It's a good way to make sure that you don't lose track of something you want to watch amid Netflix's huge library. Add something to your queue this way:

①

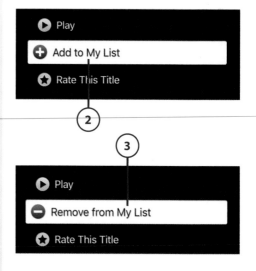

1. Find and select the item you want to add to your queue, either by searching or browsing for it.

②

2. On the details screen, highlight and select Add to My List using the remote.

③

3. That menu changes to read Remove from My List.

Now, when you return to your main Netflix screen, or select the My List menu, you'll see the item you just added at the beginning of the list.

Remove Movies and TV from Your Netflix Queue

After you've watched a movie or TV show, you might want to remove it from your queue. If so, follow these steps:

1. Find and select the movie or TV show in My List on the main screen of the app.

2. On the details screen, highlight and select Remove from My List.

3. The menu changes to read Add to My List.

With that done, the item is removed from your queue, but it's not removed from or hidden in Netflix, so you can always find it and add it again if you want.

It's Not All Good

You Can't Rearrange Your Queue on the Apple TV

Organizing your queue makes a lot of sense. You might want to put the things you want to watch next at the front or group content by genre. If you visit Netflix.com, you can do that. Unfortunately, on the Apple TV that's not possible. The Netflix app doesn't include that feature (though it does make it very easy to search and browse content). If you want to rearrange your queue, you'll have to use the Web.

Options to Watch and Control Movies and TV Shows on Netflix

When you watch a movie or TV show on Netflix, you have a number of options for controlling the video and getting more information about it. These are some of the options:

Swipe left or right on the remote touchpad to fast forward or rewind your video

Fast Forward and Reverse. Fast forward through the movie by swiping left to right on the remote's touchpad or go back by swiping right to left. When you do, a timeline and preview of what you'll see at each point in the movie appears at the bottom of the screen. When you find the point you want to jump to, click the touchpad.

Swipe down on the remote touchpad to reveal subtitle and audio controls

Subtitles. To turn on subtitles, swipe down on the remote's touchpad to reveal the Subtitles menu. Highlight the subtitles you want and click the touchpad to turn them on. Not all movies and TV shows have subtitles available.

Activate this menu by asking Siri questions about the show you're watching

Learn About Stars. To learn more about the people who made the movie or TV show, ask Siri "Who stars in this movie?" or "Who directed this movie?" A tray of results appears from the bottom of the screen. Use the remote to navigate through the results and click the touchpad to see more about any of the people. Your program automatically pauses while you check out this material.

Apple TV can display detailed information about nearly everything you watch as well as everyone involved in the production

Detail Pages. When you select a star or director, that person's page includes information about him or her from Wikipedia and other programs the person was involved in (not every person has a page). Click on any of the elements of the page to see more about the person. When you're done, click the Menu button to return to the program where you left off.

Use Siri to Control Netflix

Don't forget that the remote isn't the only way to control a movie or TV show on Netflix. You can use Siri, too. For a partial list of commands that Siri can execute for you, check out "Using Siri to Control the Apple TV" in Chapter 2, "Controlling Your Apple TV: The Remote, Siri, and Search."

How to Rate Content

One of the best things about Netflix is that it has a powerful algorithm that suggests new things you'll enjoy. This algorithm uses the behavior of millions of people—specifically what they watch and what they like—to determine what you might like. The best way to help Netflix give you better recommendations is to rate content. You can rate things you've watched on Netflix or things you've seen elsewhere, but that appear on Netflix. To rate content:

1. Find and select the item you want to rate. It could be in your queue, appear on the main screen of the app, or pop up in a search.

2. Highlight the rating category and swipe across the touchpad until you've given the item the number of stars you think it deserves.

3. Click the touchpad to save the rating. You'll know your rating has been saved because the stars turn yellow.

If you want to change your rating later, just go back to the item and select a new number of stars.

Using HBO

HBO has double the normal presence on the Apple TV: You'll find both HBO GO and HBO NOW in the Apple TV's App Store. Both of them give you access to the same library of original HBO programming and Hollywood movies. Which one is right for you depends on whether you already subscribe to HBO.

>>>*Go Further*

THE DIFFERENCE BETWEEN HBO GO AND HBO NOW

HBO offers two different services for the Apple TV, and it's important to understand which is right for you so you avoid spending money needlessly. The two HBO apps are:

- **HBO GO**—If you subscribe to HBO through your cable company, this is the app for you. The fee you pay your cable company each month for HBO covers access to HBO GO, so there's no need to pay anything else. Just log in to your cable account and you'll be all set.

- **HBO NOW**—If you don't get HBO through your cable company, but still want access to all of HBO's content, you need HBO NOW. It lets anyone subscribe to HBO directly, using Internet-connected devices to watch. For $15/month, HBO NOW gets you all of HBO's content on your Apple TV, iPhone or iPad, and other devices.

Sign In to HBO GO

If you already have HBO via your cable company, accessing HBO GO on the Apple TV is simple. You just need to add the Apple TV to your HBO account and verify that you have a subscription to start using it. Just follow these steps:

1. Launch the HBO GO app.

2. Select Activate HBO GO.

3. The app displays a website address and activation code to use to connect your provider account to your HBO GO app.

4. In a web browser on your computer or mobile device, go to the website and select Apple TV from the Select Your Device Is drop down.

5. Click Continue.

6. Browse the list of TV providers to find yours and select it.

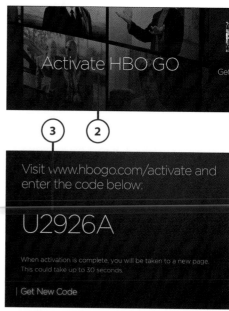

7. Log in to your provider account. Remember, this is the username and password you use to sign in at your cable company's website to pay bills and change service, not your Apple ID.

8. Enter the activation code displayed on your Apple TV screen and click Activate Device.

9. Activation success messages display in both your web browser and on the Apple TV.

10. Select the Continue link using the Apple TV remote to start using HBO GO.

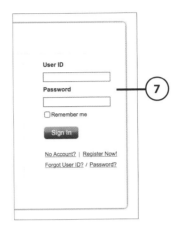

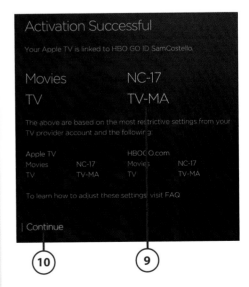

11. The main HBO GO screen appears, where you can select a show to start watching.

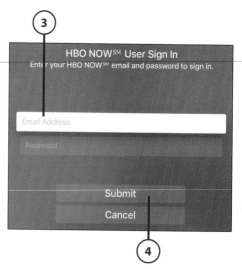

Sign In to HBO NOW

If you're already an HBO NOW subscriber, you can use your subscription on the Apple TV as soon as you sign in. Do so by following these steps:

1. Launch the HBO NOW app from the main menu of your Apple TV.

2. Select Sign In.

3. Enter your HBO NOW username and password.

4. Select the Submit button.

You're now logged in and ready to start streaming all of HBO's great Hollywood movies and original TV series and movies.

Sign Up for HBO NOW

If you don't currently get HBO and want to, you can sign up for HBO NOW directly from your Apple TV. Here's how:

1. Launch the HBO NOW app.

2. Select Start Your Free Trial.

3. Enter the email address you want to use with HBO NOW by selecting the email field and then using the onscreen keyboard or the keyboard in the Remote app to enter the address.

4. Select Done to continue.

5. Select Submit.

6. Agree to the Terms of HBO NOW by highlighting Agree and clicking the touchpad.

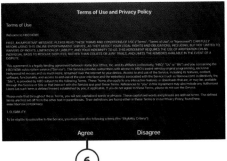

7. Your HBO NOW subscription is billed to the credit card you have on file in your Apple ID, so you're asked to log in to your Apple ID by entering your password using the onscreen keyboard.

8. Click OK.

9. The app states clearly what you're doing: subscribing to HBO NOW for $15/month after a one-month free trial. If you want to do that, select Continue.

10. The confirmation screen appears. To finalize your subscription, select OK (or Cancel if you've changed your mind).

11. You're now subscribed to HBO NOW. Select Start Watching to be delivered to the HBO NOW home screen so you can start finding content.

If You Want to Cancel

Learn more about cancelling your HBO NOW subscription, and any other subscription you set up through your Apple ID, in Chapter 5's "Manage Your Subscriptions" section. Those instructions apply only to things you sign up for using your Apple ID on Apple TV, an iOS device, or iTunes. If you subscribed in another way, you'll have to cancel on the service's website.

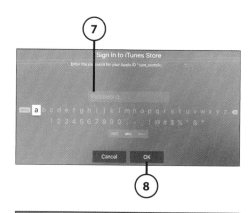

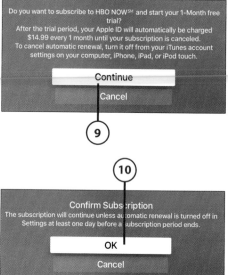

Finding Content in HBO Apps

Although HBO doesn't have a library as big as Netflix's, it regularly features some of the most prestigious and talked-about TV series and movies. Because its library is smaller, finding content is relatively easy—and, as usual, you can browse and search.

Siri Works Here, Too

Just like with Netflix, HBO's apps are included in the Apple TV's universal search. So, any time you use Siri to search for content, if HBO has it, you'll know.

Searching for content in HBO apps is pretty straightforward—select the Search menu and type in whatever you're looking for—browsing isn't much more complicated:

1. Launch your preferred HBO app.

2. The home screen of both apps displays various featured movies and TV series drawn from a number of genres.

3. If you don't see what you're looking for there, select one of the categories on the left-hand side of the screen (for the purposes of this tutorial, I'm using Series).

4. The contents of that category appear on the main screen in alphabetical order. Swipe side to side and up and down on the remote to navigate through the content of that section. The remote's Menu button takes you back a step.

5. When you've found something you're interested in, select it using the remote to see more information.

Add Items to the Watchlist

Just like Netflix has its queue where you can save content to watch in the future, HBO's Watchlist performs the same function. To add items to it:

1. Find the content you want to add by searching or browsing.

2. Select the item you're interested in.

3. On the item's detail screen, highlight and select the + Watchlist button.

4. To access the items you add to your Watchlist, go to the main screen of the HBO app and select Watchlist from the top of the menu on the left.

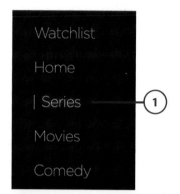

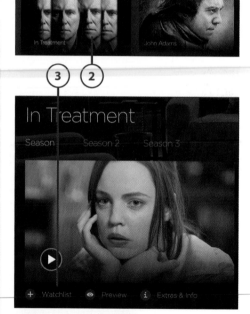

Options to Watch and Control Movies and TV on HBO

When you're watching a movie or TV show from HBO, the apps offer a handful of options, including:

Swipe left or right on the remote touchpad to fast forward or reverse your video

Fast Forward and Reverse. To move forward through a program, swipe left to right across the touchpad. The faster you swipe, the faster you'll move. To reverse, swipe right to left. Click the touchpad to start watching again.

Remember, you can use Siri to do this, too, by saying things like "move forward 10 minutes."

Swipe down on the remote touchpad to reveal subtitle and audio controls

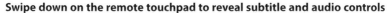

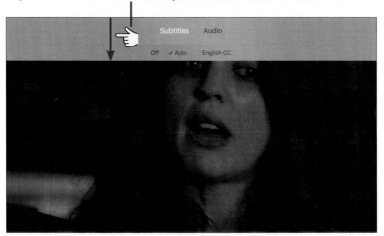

Subtitles. To turn on subtitles (when they're available), swipe down on the touchpad when watching something. On the menu that appears, use the remote to highlight the option you want and click the touchpad to start using it.

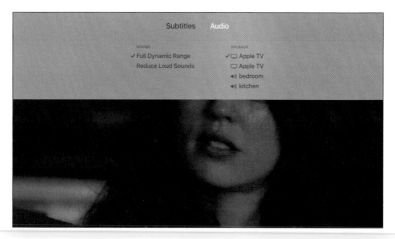

Audio. Swipe down on the touchpad and select the Audio option to access a pair of audio settings. The first allows you to choose either the full sound of the program you're watching or to reduce loud noise so that dialogue is easier to hear. The second lets you choose the speakers you're sending the audio to.

Activate this menu by asking Siri questions about the show you're watching

Learn About Stars. Just like in other apps, you can learn about the people who made the program you're watching. Just ask Siri "Who stars in this?" or "Who directed this?" A tray of basic information appears at the bottom of the screen. To learn more about these people, select them using the remote.

Using Showtime

HBO isn't the only premiere cable network with a dual presence on the Apple TV. Showtime does the same thing with its Showtime Anytime app, which is for people who subscribe to the channel via cable and satellite providers, and Showtime—its Internet streaming app/service—which you can subscribe to directly without a conventional TV provider.

Sign In To Showtime Anytime

If you subscribe to Showtime through your cable or satellite provider, follow these steps to watch Showtime on the Apple TV:

1. Install and launch the Showtime Anytime app.

2. In the menu across the top of the screen, select Settings (you might need to swipe up the touchpad to reveal the menu).

3. Select Activate Showtime Anytime.

4. Swipe up and down on the touchpad to locate and select your cable or satellite provider (if your provider isn't listed here, you might not be able to access Showtime Anytime; check with them).

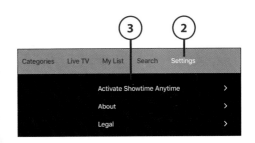

5. The app displays an activation code. Make note of it; you'll need to enter it on the Showtime Anytime website.

6. In a web browser on a mobile device or computer, go to http://www.showtimeanytime.com/activate.

7. Select Apple TV from the drop-down menu.

8. Enter the activation code from step 5 in the box and click Activate.

9. A confirmation appears in the web browser and on the Apple TV. On the Apple TV, select Continue.

10. After activation, the first screen you see is the main Settings screen of Showtime Anytime. Click the Menu button until you get back to the main screen or swipe up to reveal the top navigation and select Showtime Anytime.

Sign In To Showtime Streaming

If you subscribe to Showtime's streaming service, you can use your subscription on the Apple TV, too. Just install the app, and then follow these instructions:

1. Launch Showtime.

2. Select Already Subscribed? Sign In.

Subscribe Now

If you want to start a new subscription, select Start Your 30-Day Free Trial instead and follow the on-screen instructions (see the next section).

---

3. Use the onscreen keyboard or the Remote app to enter your Showtime account username and select Next.

4. Enter your Showtime account password and select Sign In.

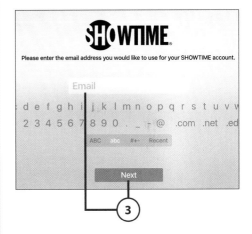

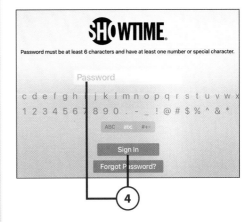

5. With that done, you're delivered to the app's main screen and can start looking for something to watch.

Restore an iTunes Purchase

If you subscribed to Showtime streaming through your Apple ID on another device, such as an iPad or computer, choose the Purchased Through iTunes? Restore Now option in Step 2 of the tutorial above. This connects your existing subscription to your Apple TV.

Sign Up For Showtime Streaming

You might not subscribe to Showtime by any means right now, but if you want to change that and sign up for Showtime's streaming service, you can do so right on the Apple TV. As with other subscriptions on the Apple TV, the credit card on file in your Apple ID is billed each month. Here's how:

1. Launch Showtime.

2. Select Start Your 30-Day Free Trial.

3. Enter the email address you want to use for your subscription. This doubles as the username you use for signing into the service.

4. Click Next.

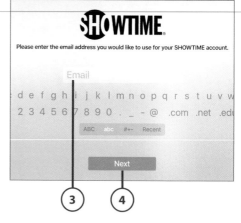

5. Enter the password you want to use for this account. (The app will let you know if you need to make your password more secure.)

6. Click Sign In.

7. You need to accept the service's Terms of Use to subscribe. Select the I Accept button.

8. This screen explains the details of what you're agreeing to: You're paying $10.99, billed to your Apple ID, every month. Assuming you still want to subscribe, select Continue.

9. Your last chance before the subscription starts. If you've changed your mind, select Cancel. Otherwise, select OK.

10. Your free trial has started. Click Start Watching to begin finding content to enjoy.

Cancelling Your Subscription

Remember, if you subscribed to Showtime on the Apple TV, you can cancel your subscription on it, too. For instructions on how to do that, check out "Managing In-App Purchases and Subscriptions" in Chapter 5.

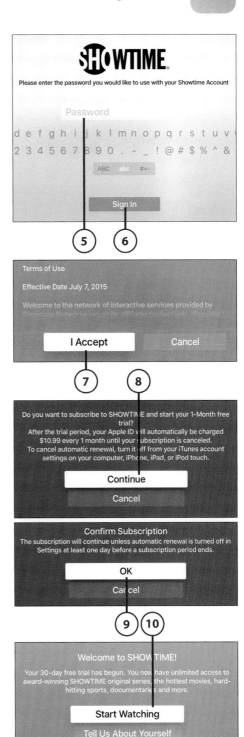

Finding Content In Showtime Apps

Whichever Showtime app you use, finding things to watch works the same way:

1. Launch your preferred Showtime app.

2. There are four ways to find content, the first of which is by browsing the featured items on the main screen. Swipe up and down and left and right to find programs. When you find one you're interested in, select it and skip to step 9.

3. Another way to find content is by browsing categories. To do this, select Categories in the menu at the top of the screen.

4. The right-hand menu lists all the categories of content available in the app. Select one you're interested in to see its main screen.

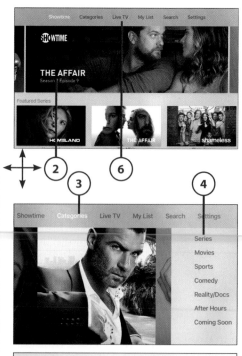

5. On the Categories screen, you can filter by current or past series and browse series. When you find one that looks interesting, select it and skip to step 9.

6. By choosing the Live TV menu at the top of the screen, you can tune in to whatever's being broadcast on Showtime right now.

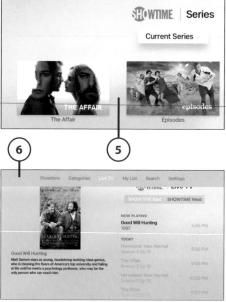

7. Lastly, if you know exactly what you're looking for, search for it. Begin by selecting the Search menu at the top of the screen.

8. Using the onscreen keyboard, type what you're looking for. As you type, results will appear below.

9. Swipe down on the touchpad to navigate the results. Select the item you'd like to see more about.

10. On the detail screen for the item (a season of a TV series is shown here), you can select individual episodes, learn more about a series or movie, and start watching.

Add Items to My List

If you've found something you want to watch, but don't want to watch right now, you can save it to your My List. Just follow these instructions:

1. Browse or search your preferred Showtime app to find the content you want. Select the item to see its detail screen.

2. For movies, you'll go right to the detail screen. For TV series, you'll go to a series overview screen. Select the episode you want to add to your list.

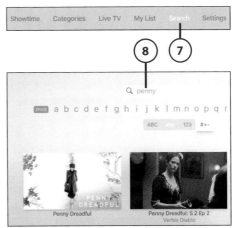

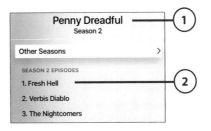

3. On the movie or TV episode detail screen, select Add.

4. A confirmation message pops up to let you know the item is now in your list. Select OK to continue.

5. Access your list by selecting My List from the menu at the top of the screen.

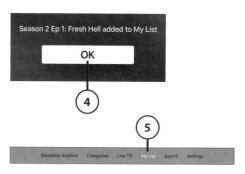

Options to Watch and Control Movies and TV on Showtime

Both Showtime apps offer you the following options for controlling and learning about movies and TV while they're playing:

Swipe left or right on the remote touchpad to fast forward or reverse your video

Fast Forward and Reverse. The Apple TV makes it easy to move back and forth through the movies and TV episodes you're watching. You can use Siri to move precisely (try commands like "skip forward 90 seconds") or the touchpad to move fluidly. Swipe left to right to fast forward and right to left to reverse. Click the touchpad to start playing at the new location.

Swipe down on the remote touchpad to reveal subtitles

Subtitles. To enable subtitles for the program you're already watching, swipe down on the touchpad to reveal the tray and select Subtitles. Select one of the available subtitle options to turn it on.

Don't Forget Siri

Just like with fast forward and reverse, most Siri commands that have been covered elsewhere work here. Use Siri to turn on subtitles, to learn about directors and actors, and more.

The swipe-down menu also contains Audio options

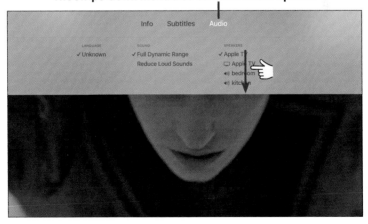

Audio. You can also control the audio playback for the program you're watching. Swipe down to reveal the tray and select Audio. In that section, you can choose to watch in another language (if one is available), to boost dialogue and reduce sound effects with Reduce Loud Sounds, or change the speakers the audio is sent to in the Speakers menu.

Using Hulu

Hulu is slightly different from Netflix and HBO; it's a service focused almost entirely on TV (it has a relatively small selection of movies, though some—like the Criterion Collection—are very high quality), which makes sense because it is owned and run by Disney/ABC, Fox, and NBCUniversal.

The service is great for binge-watchers; you'll find lots of full seasons of new and classic shows, as well as full-series runs of shows like The X-Files, Buffy the Vampire Slayer, and South Park.

Hulu is one of the best ways to see new TV shows if you don't have cable. New episodes are usually posted the day after they're broadcast and the service usually has the last five episodes of big-name shows, and often more than that for others. The major downside of Hulu compared to the other services examined in this chapter, so far, is that it includes a fairly large amount of advertising in its lowest price subscription; an ad-free option costs more.

It's Not All Good

No Free Hulu on Apple TV

If you're familiar with Hulu, you know that its website offers a totally free version which, in exchange for viewing ads, lets you watch a limited selection of its library. Despite the free option existing on the Web, it's never been offered on the iPhone or iPad, and the same is true here. If you want to use Hulu on the Apple TV, you'll have to pay for it.

Sign In to Your Hulu Account

If you already have a Hulu subscription, using it on the Apple TV is simple. Just install the Hulu app and follow these steps to sign in:

1. Launch the Hulu app.

2. Navigate to and select Log In using the touchpad.

3. Enter your Hulu username and password.

4. Select Log In.

5. The Hulu home screen appears, where you can browse or search for new content, check out episodes of series you already watch, get recommendations, or pick something from your queue.

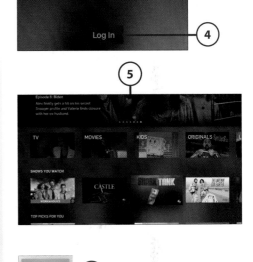

Subscribe to Hulu

Are you new to Hulu, but ready to sign up? With its 30-day free trial, you're not risking much. Here's what you need to do to get started:

1. Launch the Hulu app.

2. Highlight and select Start Your Free Trial using the remote.

3. Hulu gives you a 30-day free trial, but you need to choose the kind of plan you want when the trial is over. Use the remote to highlight the one you prefer and select it by clicking the touchpad.

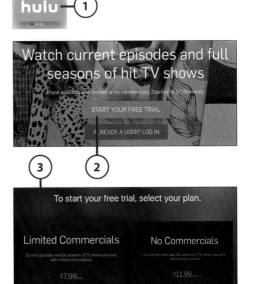

4. Fill out the form with the required information.

5. After completing the form, select Create My Account.

6. This screen provides the specific details of what you're subscribing to and what you'll pay. Select Continue to proceed.

7. The confirmation screen is the final step before your free trial and subscription begin. If you've changed your mind and don't want to subscribe, select Cancel. To start your subscription, select OK.

8. The Hulu app home screen appears, where you can start finding TV and movies to enjoy.

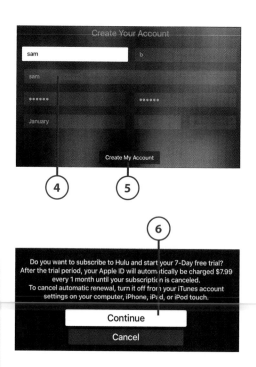

Subscription Management

Just like with the other apps discussed earlier in the chapter, if you sign up for Hulu using your Apple ID, your monthly subscription will be billed to the credit card you have on file in your Apple ID and you can manage your subscription using the steps outlined in "Manage Your Subscriptions" in Chapter 5.

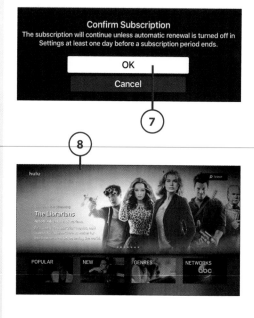

Find Content in Hulu

Apple TV's universal search feature also combs through Hulu to see whether it offers what you're looking for. So, the easiest way to find things in Hulu is searching with Siri, though the app offers its own search, too.

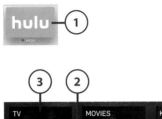

If you prefer to browse Hulu to see what it has to offer, follow these steps:

1. Launch the Hulu app.

2. The first screen in the app shows you featured releases, programs you watch regularly (if you've used Hulu before), and recommended items. Navigate by swiping up and down, left and right on the touchpad.

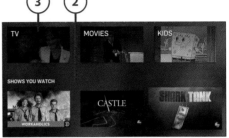

3. Select a category to see the content it contains.

4. If you select the TV category, the screen that appears includes featured TV programs at the top and subcategories below. Use the remote to navigate the screen and the touchpad to get more detail on a program or category.

5. The main screen of the movies category works the same way as for TV: featured items on top and subcategories below. Select items to see more.

6. If you know exactly what you're looking for, you can search for it. Use the remote to highlight the Search box in the top-right corner of the screen. Select it by clicking the touchpad.

7. On the Search screen, use the onscreen keyboard to type in what you're looking for. As you type, suggested results appear just above the letters you input. When you see something you're interested in, use the remote to highlight the suggestion.

8. With the suggestion highlighted, information about the show displays at the top of the screen.

9. Select the image to go to the item's detail page, or choose to watch the latest episode or add it to your favorites.

10. When you select a search result, the main screen for the TV series or movie appears. On this screen are options for watching the latest episode, seeing a list of all episodes, watching clips, adding the show to favorites, and more. Use the remote to select the option that appeals to you.

Enter text

Select suggested results

Options to Watch and Control Movies and TV Shows on Hulu

After you've started watching a TV episode or movie on Hulu, you have these options for controlling it:

Swipe left or right on the remote touchpad to fast forward or rewind your video

Fast Forward and Reverse. As with Netflix and HBO, swiping left to right moves forward in the program, and swiping right to left moves backward. The faster you swipe, the faster the video moves. Click the touchpad to jump to the new location.

Swipe down on the remote touchpad to reveal subtitle and audio controls

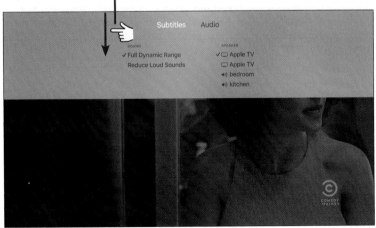

Subtitles. To turn on subtitles, where they are available, swipe down on the touchpad and select an option from the Subtitles menu.

Audio. When you swipe down on the touchpad, you can also access the Audio menu. The first option lets you reduce the volume of sound effects to make dialogue easier to hear, whereas the second lets you choose what speakers the audio should play through.

It's Not All Good

Hulu Doesn't Support Some Siri Features

When you're using Hulu, you can't ask Siri who directed or stars in a program. Hulu doesn't support that feature (as of this writing, at least). It's up to each app to support that feature and provide that information to Siri. Hulu, it seems, doesn't do that right now.

Video Apps to Check Out

The video apps covered in this chapter barely scratch the surface of the bountiful selection of video apps you'll find in the App Store. If you want to explore some alternative sources of great entertainment, check out these video apps:

Daily Burn—The Apple TV doesn't have to just be about sitting on the couch. With Daily Burn, it can also be the center of your home workout routine. This app provides all kinds of guided exercises that you can do at home, for varying levels of athleticism. You'll spend $13/month, but that's less than many gym memberships.

Funny Or Die—If you love to laugh, you'll love Funny Or Die. This popular comedy website from Will Ferrell and writer/director Adam McKay offers tons of hilarious short video series, such as Zack Galifianakis' Between Two Ferns or Billy Eichner's Billy on the Street. The videos here are free.

MLB.com At Bat—Fans of America's Pastime will want to check out MLB.com At Bat when the season starts. If you have a subscription, the app delivers streaming video of games, live look-ins, video clips, an archive of classic games, and more. Among the coolest features are breaking news notifications to alert you to check out no-hitters, perfect games, and lead changes.

NBA League Pass—This app does for basketball fans a lot of what MLB does for baseball fans: provides access to hundreds and hundreds of games from every team in the league. Subscriptions cost $120–$200, depending on how many teams' games you want to watch. Do you want to check out the best games, but don't have the time? Try the condensed game feature, which delivers the key plays of each game in less time.

TED—If you want your television watching to be educational and thought provoking, not just entertaining, this app full of TED Talks is a great option. This collection of free videos lets you browse based on your interests, check out videos that are popular with others, and have random videos play to introduce you to topics you might not know you're interested in.

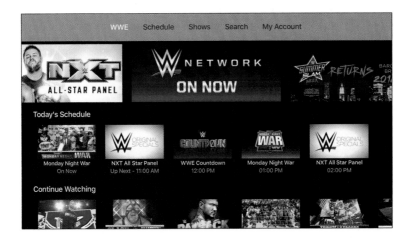

WWE Network—There aren't games in the same way as with the other sports apps, but the WWE network delivers tons of wrestling to fans for just $9.99/month. Not only does it have all the WWE's weekly shows, but it also sports thousands of hours of vintage matches, and gives you access to all the major events each year, including WrestleMania. As the saying goes, "It's not fake sports, it's real entertainment."

YouTube—No collection of online video apps is complete without the grand-daddy of them all: YouTube. You can find virtually anything on YouTube, from original series to music to old movies and more. And given that users upload one hour of new video to YouTube every second, you'll never run out of things to watch.

Enhance the Apple TV's range of entertainment
options by installing new apps and games.

Although the Apple TV might be stocked with a bunch of useful pre-installed apps, you can expand the functionality and fun of the device by installing apps from the App Store. In this chapter, you'll learn about:

→ Finding apps and games

→ Downloading and managing apps

→ Playing games on the Apple TV

→ Managing in-app purchases and subscriptions

→ Updating apps to new versions

→ Apps to check out

Using Apps and Games

If you have an iPhone or iPad, you know that the built-in apps are useful, but the apps and games you get at the App Store are what make your device so powerful, indispensable, and fun. The same is true of the Apple TV: It has its own App Store that takes the device far beyond the pre-installed apps. Some of your favorite iPhone and iPad apps will probably show up in the Apple TV App Store, but there will also be some new apps that you won't be able to live without.

Apps for the Apple TV are designed especially for use on an HDTV from across the room. They're also made to be controlled using Siri and the Siri Remote.

Finding Apps and Games

The App Store app on the Apple TV works basically the same way as it does on the iPhone or iPad. You can search for apps or browse the store; some apps are free, some require upfront payment, others have in-app purchases.

Search the Apple TV App Store

If you know the name of the app you're looking for, follow these steps to search for it:

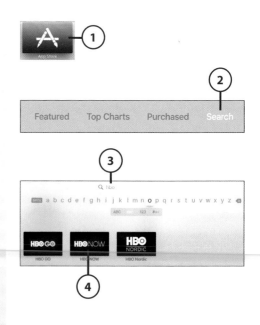

1. Launch the App Store app.

2. Use the touchpad to navigate to and select Search.

3. Type in what you're searching for using the onscreen keyboard or the Remote app. Results of your search automatically populate beneath the keyboard.

4. When you've found an app you're interested in, highlight it using the remote and click the touchpad to learn more about it and download it.

Browse the Apple TV App Store

If you don't know what you're looking for or just prefer to peruse what's out there in hopes of discovering something new, you can also browse the App Store. Here's how:

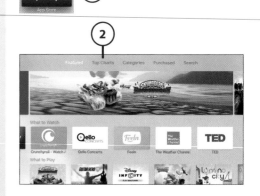

1. Launch the App Store app.

2. The main screen of the app displays Featured apps based on categories and promotional groups assembled by Apple. You can navigate to any of these using the touchpad or the Remote app; click to select them.

3. The Top Charts screen shows the apps that are most popular in categories like paid apps, free apps, and the apps that have generated the most money.

4. Use the top navigation to select Categories.

5. Select one of the categories in the right-hand menu to view highlighted apps in that category.

6. To view any apps you've purchased or downloaded in the past, select the Purchased menu in the top navigation.

7. Select one of the categories on the left.

8. The apps in the category you chose are displayed on the right. Use the remote to navigate to and select the app you want.

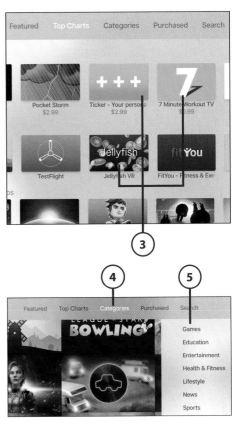

All About the App Detail Screen

When you select an app to learn more about it, the screen that appears contains this information:

1. **Title**—The name of the app.

2. **Developer**—The person or company who created the app.

3. **Category**—The App Store category that the app is assigned to.

4. **Age Rating**—The minimum appropriate age for users of the app, according to the developer.

5. **Star Rating**—The average of all the star ratings assigned to the app by other users.

6. **Description**—The developer's overview of what the app is, what it does, and who it's for.

7. **In-App Purchases**—Indicates whether you can purchase items, upgrades, or other features in the game. See "Managing In-App Purchases and Subscriptions" later in this chapter (optional, not pictured).

8. **Get/Buy Button**—Use this button if you're ready to download the app. For free apps, the button reads "Get." Paid apps show the price.

9. **Screenshots**—To get a sense of what the app looks like before downloading it (especially useful for games and paid apps), check out its screenshots.

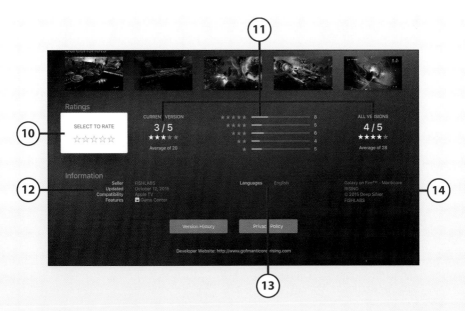

10. **Rate App**—If you've used the app and want to let others know what you think of it, use this area to assign a star rating. For instructions on how to do that, see "Review Apps at the App Store" later in this chapter.

11. **Ratings**—The ratings represent what other users think of the app. This section displays the current star rating, the number of ratings, and how many times each star rating has been assigned. You'll see those reviews for both the current version of the app and all versions, for all time.

12. **Information**—Basic information about the app, such as when it was last updated and whether it offers features like Game Center support (for more on Game Center, check out "Playing Games on the Apple TV" later in this chapter).

13. **Languages**—The languages in which the game is available.

14. **Credits**—Legal information about the developer of the app.

Downloading and Managing Apps

After you find an app that appeals to you, download it. The process is fairly similar whether you're buying it or getting a free app, but after you get an app, there's a lot to learn.

You Need an Apple ID

Back in Chapter 1, "Introduction to Your Apple TV," I covered how to set up an Apple ID. This is one of those situations in which you use it. You use the credit card on file in your Apple ID to pay for apps you buy. Even if you're downloading a free app, you need to be logged in to your Apple ID to complete the download.

How to Buy Apps

After you've browsed or searched the App Store and found an app you want to try, follow these steps to get it on your Apple TV:

1. On the app detail screen, use the remote to highlight and select the Get/Buy button.

2. You might be asked to log in to your Apple ID. If you are, do so. If you're downloading a free app, the app begins to download. You can skip to step 4 or 5.

3. If you're buying an app, this screen makes sure that you understand that you're about to buy and download an app. If you've changed your mind, select Cancel. Otherwise, select Buy.

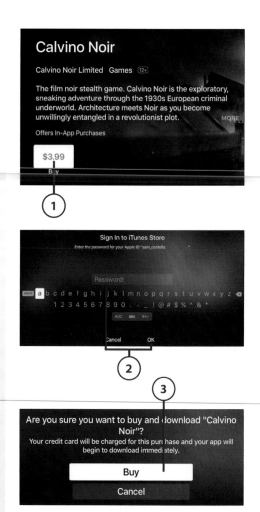

4. When you purchase and download the app, the Buy button on
the app detail screen changes
to Open. Highlight it and click
the touchpad on the remote to
launch the app.

5. When the app finishes downloading, it appears on the home
screen of your Apple TV. You can
launch it using Siri or the remote.

You Can't Rent Apps

Just like you can't rent TV shows using
iTunes, you can't rent apps at the App
Store. A lot of apps are free, so rental
wouldn't apply to them, but Apple
doesn't allow rentals for paid apps. It
makes sense—how would you figure
out how much a rental should cost and
how long it would last? Luckily, most
apps are relatively cheap (common price
points are $5 or less) so even an app you
end up not liking isn't much of a loss.

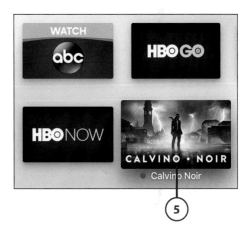

Stop Having to Enter Your Password for Every Download

The onscreen keyboard for entering
your Apple ID password can be pretty
hard to use, especially if you have a long
or complex password. Using the keyboard in the Remote app is easier, but
not as easy as skipping typing entirely.
Luckily, a setting can save you from having to do either. In fact, you can set it so
that you never have to enter your password again. Just follow these steps:

1. Launch the Settings app.

2. Select Accounts.

3. Select iTunes and App Store.

4. Select Password Settings.

5. In the Purchases and In-App Purchases section, select the Require Password menu.

6. Choose how often you want to have to enter your password when you download or purchase things at the iTunes and App Stores: Always (that is, every time), After 15 Minutes, or Never. Highlight your choice and select it by clicking the touchpad.

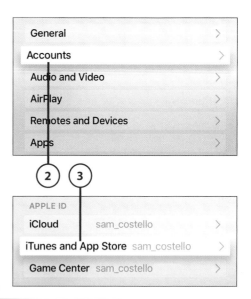

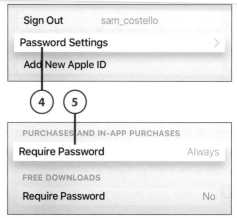

7. Type in your password to authorize and save the change. Click OK.

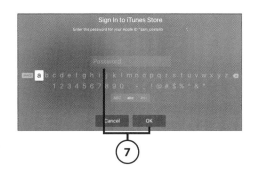

⑦

Words of Warning

One thing to keep in mind: You might not want to use this option if you have kids who use the Apple TV. With this setting, they'll be able to buy as many games, in-app purchases, or other apps as they like.

>>>Go Further

PASSWORD SETTINGS FOR FREE APPS

There's no reason to enter your password every time you download a free app. After all, it doesn't cost you anything. The Apple TV knows that and by default doesn't require you to enter your password. If you want to change that setting, follow all the steps in the last tutorial and then toggle the Require Password menu to No in the Free Downloads section.

Delete Apps

If you've downloaded an app, tried it out, and found that you don't like it or it doesn't do what you need, you can delete it. Here's how:

①

1. Highlight the app you want to delete using the remote and click and hold down the remote's touchpad.

2. When the prompt appears at the bottom of the screen, press the Play/Pause button on the remote.

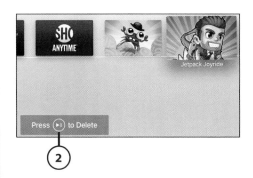

②

3. This screen ensures that you know what you're doing. If you've changed your mind, select Cancel. If you still want to delete the app, select Delete.

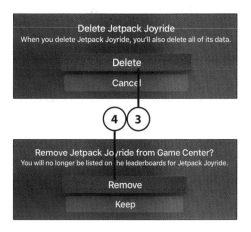

4. Some games store data related to your progress, achievements, and scores in Game Center. Decide whether you want to remove all of that data from Game Center or keep it for later access. Highlight your choice and select it by clicking the touchpad.

The app is now removed from your Apple TV. For another approach to deleting apps and other data, check out "Manage Your Storage" later in this chapter.

>>>Go Further

REDOWNLOAD PREVIOUS APP PURCHASES

If you've downloaded an app—whether free or paid—you can download it again for no extra charge. (Assuming that the app is still available in the App Store, that is. If the developer has stopped offering it, you won't be able to download it again.) This can come in handy if an app that you previously deleted has been updated with major new features or if you accidentally deleted something. Either way, redownload your previous app purchases from the Purchased section of the App Store app. For more, check out "Browse the Apple TV App Store" earlier in this chapter.

Requesting Refunds for Paid Apps

If you buy an app and it doesn't work properly or you feel you were misled into buying it, you might want to request a refund from Apple. To log this request, follow these steps:

1. On your computer or mobile device, open your web browser and go to http://reportaproblem. apple.com.

2. Type your Apple ID and password, and click Sign In.

3. Locate the purchase for which you want a refund and click the Report a Problem button next to it.

Sorting Purchases
You can sort your list of purchases using the buttons at the top of screen.

---

4. Choose the reason for the refund from the drop-down menu and add any notes you want (notes are optional).

5. Highlight and click the Submit button to send the request.

Refund Not Guaranteed
Requesting a refund is trickier than it sounds: Apple is fairly stingy when it comes to issuing refunds. This is because you still get to keep and use the app after getting a refund, so there's a possibility for misuse. Now, you'll just have to wait to see whether Apple will refund your money. Fingers crossed!

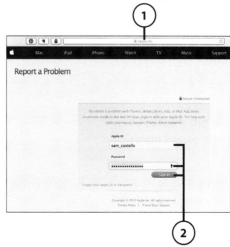

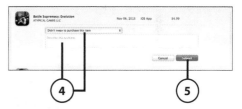

>>>Go Further

STREAMING APPS AND GAMES

Here's a cool trivia tidbit about apps on the Apple TV: When you download one, you don't always download the entire thing. Take games, for instance. Because games need so much high-quality video and audio, they can be huge downloads. But rather than make you wait for gigabytes to download, the Apple TV intelligently downloads the first few levels of the game now, and then downloads later levels as you need them using a technology called "app slicing." It's just one more way the Apple TV gets you using the apps and games you love faster.

Manage Your Storage

Even though the Apple TV offers a lot of storage space—32GB or 64GB, depending on which model you bought—it can fill up quickly. If you cram it full of apps, games in particular, your device could run low on space. One way to free up space is to delete apps, but if you want to get a good sense of what's taking up all that space before you start deleting, learn how to manage your storage. Here's what you need to do:

1. Launch Settings.

2. Select General.

3. In the Usage section, select Manage Storage.

4. The Manage Storage screen shows all the items that are taking up space on your Apple TV. This includes only apps that you've downloaded from the App Store, not the built-in apps that come with the Apple TV.

5. To delete an item from this screen, use the remote to highlight and select the trash can next to the item you want to delete.

6. In the screen that appears, select Delete to complete the deletion; select Cancel if you've changed your mind.

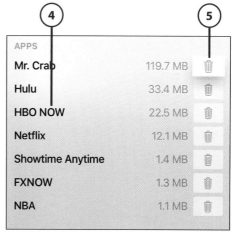

It's Not All Good

You Can't Delete Built-In Apps

You can delete any app you download from the App Store, but if you really need to free up storage space or just don't like to look at apps you don't use, you might want to delete the device's built-in apps, such as iTunes TV Shows, Computers, or Photos.

Bad news: You can't. Just like on the iPhone and iPad, you can't remove the apps that come pre-loaded on the Apple TV.

Review Apps at the App Store

Do you love an app and want to give positive feedback to the developer? Are you totally frustrated by a game and feel the need to warn others? You should review it at the App Store. Your review takes the form of a star rating. Follow these steps to rate an app:

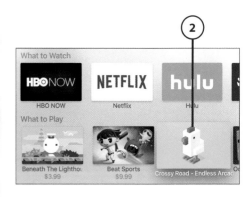

1. Launch the App Store app.

2. Search for and select the app you want to review (or find it in your Purchased menu).

3. In the Ratings section, highlight and click on Select to Rate.

4. Select the number of stars you think the app deserves by swiping across the touchpad and clicking to confirm the rating.

5. The app's detail screen shows your rating applied in the Select to Rate box. Follow these steps again if you want to change your rating.

Ratings

SELECT TO RATE

★★★ ★ ★

CURRENT VERSION

4.5 / 5

★★★★✦

Average of 86

Information

Seller	Hipster Whale Pty Ltd
Updated	October 27, 2015
Compatibility	Apple TV, iPhone, iPad, iPod touch
Languages	English

5

It's Not All Good

You Can't Write Reviews on the Apple TV

If you've used other Apple products to review apps or videos, you know that in many cases you can do more than just leave a star rating—you can also write a text review. Not on the Apple TV, though. On it, you can only leave star reviews. This makes sense: You wouldn't want to try to type out a lengthy review using the Apple TV's somewhat unwieldy onscreen keyboard. So, if you want to write a review, you'll need to use your computer or mobile device.

Playing Games on the Apple TV

In some ways, games on the Apple TV are just like any other kind of app: You get them at the App Store; Some are free, some are paid; they include in-app purchases; and you install and delete them in the same way. In other ways, though, they're very different: They require that you use the remote in new ways, they let you play with your friends around the world, and some can let you pick up playing on another device where you left off on the Apple TV.

You won't find the latest big-name releases for the PlayStation or Xbox on the Apple TV (at least not on the same day they're released for the major consoles; sometimes they come out for Apple devices later), but enough fun, challenging games are available to keep you busy for hours, days, and weeks.

>>>Go Further

KEEP ON PLAYING WITH CROSS-DEVICE GAMES

Imagine playing a game on your iPhone during your commute home and then being able to pick up right where you left off in that game on your Apple TV when you get home.

If you have games that are available for the iPhone and/or iPad *and* the Apple TV, and if the developer of the game has added support for this feature, all of your devices will automatically be aware of your progress and will allow you to continue your game no matter on which device you're playing.

Check your favorite games to see whether they support this cool bonus.

Use the Siri Remote to Play Games

For most Apple TV owners, the first way you play games is by using the Siri remote to control them. All you need to do is launch a game and then flip the remote sideways and—thanks to the accelerometer and gyroscope in it being able to understand how you're holding it—you'll be ready to play games.

Here's what you need to know about what the remote's buttons do when you're playing games:

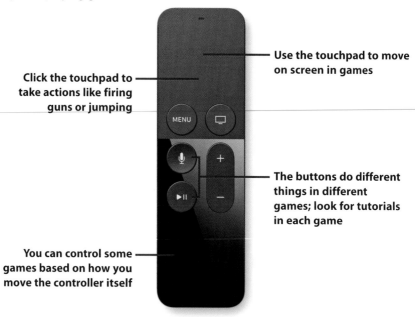

Click the touchpad to take actions like firing guns or jumping

Use the touchpad to move on screen in games

The buttons do different things in different games; look for tutorials in each game

You can control some games based on how you move the controller itself

- The controls are different for each game. You'll always use the touchpad and the buttons, but what they do isn't consistent from game to game. Most games have tutorial modes or onscreen instructions. Look for those to learn how to use the remote for them.

- The touchpad is directional. In most cases, you'll move through the game using the touchpad. Just like you swipe around apps and menus, you'll move your character or other onscreen elements in games with the touchpad.

- Click the touchpad to take action. Clicking the touchpad in games does things like fire guns, jump, or take other in-game actions.

- Some games respond to the movement of the controller itself. Remember, the controller has an accelerometer and gyroscope in it, meaning that it can detect how you're holding it and moving it. Some games respond to the movement of the remote, like on the Nintendo Wii.

Use Third-Party Game Controllers

If you or someone in your household is really into games, third-party game controllers probably make sense for you. These controllers look and function more like the controllers that come with the PlayStation or Xbox and give you different sorts of control options.

It's not possible to provide a specific tutorial because so many controllers are available, each of which has a different configuration of buttons and options, so games might work slightly differently with each controller.

One useful thing to know is that after you've paired a game controller with your Apple TV, it can perform almost all the functions of the Siri Remote. Game controllers can navigate through menus and screens, select items, launch apps, and more. The only function a game controller can't mirror is using Siri to control the TV by voice.

Connecting Third-Party Controllers

For instructions on how to connect a third-party controller to your Apple TV, see "How to Connect a Third-Party Game Controller to Apple TV" in Chapter 2, "Controlling Your Apple TV: "The Remote, Siri, and Search.""

Sign In to Game Center

Game Center is an Apple service that lets you track the games you play and your high scores and achievements in them, connect with friends, play turn-based games, and even play multiplayer games over the Internet. If you've played many games on the iPhone, iPad, or Mac, you might have some experience with Game Center. It's almost identical on the Apple TV—and it's built in to the operating system.

If you have a Game Center account that uses your Apple ID, when you sign into your Apple ID on the Apple TV, you automatically sign in to the Game Center account, too. If you need to sign in to the account separately, though, follow these steps:

1. Launch Settings.

2. Select Accounts.

3. Select Game Center.

4. Select Sign in to Game Center.

5. Sign in to the Apple ID you use for your Game Center account and click Continue.

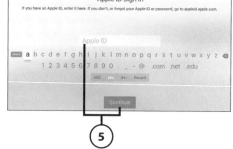

6. You'll know you're signed in when the menu changes to read Sign Out and shows your username. (Do not click this option unless you intend to sign out.)

>>>Go Further
CONTROL GAME CENTER INVITATIONS

One of the things Game Center is best for is connecting to people who play the same games as you so you can play head to head. However, you might prefer to only play solo and not connect to others. In that case, you should turn off the ability to receive game invitations. To do that, follow the first four steps in the last tutorial. On the Game Center screen, toggle the Allow Invites menu to Off.

Use Game Center to Check Scores

One of the fun things about Game Center is that it allows you to see the high scores in the games you play from players all around the world. This is a great way to see where you stack up or to find other players to challenge to head-to-head matches (assuming the game you play supports that, of course).

Different games provide different ways to access these scores, and not all games provide them, but look for menus called Scores or Game Center and you'll be on the right track.

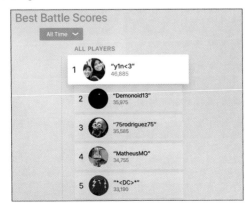

Challenge Friends to Games

Video games that you play on your own are fun, but the ones where you can play your friends—especially friends who live far away—are even better. Game Center makes it easy for you to challenge your friends to a match—assuming they have Game Center accounts and you're friends in Game Center. Those are both requirements. Not all games, even ones that use Game Center, support this feature and no single tutorial can cover every kind of game.

That said, here's an example of how one game—10 Pin Shuffle—handles head-to-head challenges. It provides a solid foundation to help you understand how other games might provide the same challenge-your-friends feature:

1. Launch the game you want to play with your friend.

2. Find the Scores or Game Center menu and select it.

3. Find an achievement or score in the game and select it.

4. Select Challenge Friends.

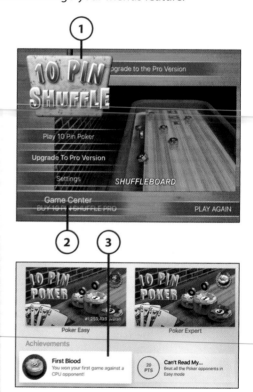

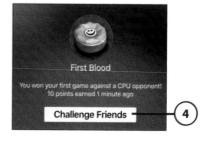

5. Choose the friend you want to play with from the list.

6. Click the Send button to challenge your friend and start playing (assuming he or she is online and accepts, that is).

It's Not All Good

No Friend Invitations on Apple TV

The iOS and Mac versions of Game Center enable you to find friends and send them invitations to connect and play games together. No similar feature exists on the Apple TV. You can access the friends you already have, but can't connect to new ones. You'll need to use your Mac or iOS device for that.

Use Game Center for Multiplayer Gaming

Besides one-on-one matchups, Game Center supports multiplayer gaming with both your friends and other Game Center users whom you don't know. Using this feature can be a great way to test your skills against other players worldwide and maybe even connect to people with similar interests.

Like other Game Center features, the exact way you use multiplayer gaming depends on the game. Not all games support it, and the ones that do have different ways of letting you join multiplayer games. This tutorial, using a paper airplane–flying game called Air Wings, gives a useful, though not universal, example:

1. Launch the game.

2. Look for and select the option to start the game.

3. Look for and select its multiplayer option.

4. If offered, choose the number of players you want to compete with and click the touchpad.

5. Game Center gives you two options: play with strangers it finds for you, or play with your Game Center friends. To play with strangers, select Play Now. To play against your friends, select Invite Players.

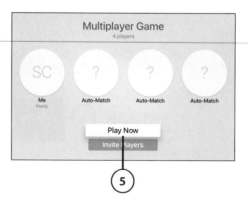

6. If you select Play Now, Game Center looks for other players who have the game open and are looking for a multiplayer game to join. As it finds players and they join your game, they appear on the screen.

7. When all players are ready, Game Center connects you all into the same game session and starts you playing.

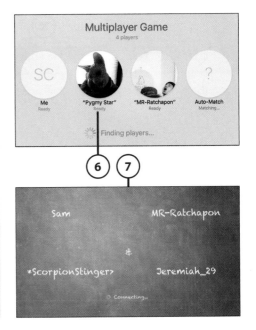

It's Not All Good

Only One Remote at a Time Can Control Games

The Apple TV makes using the Siri Remote to control games easy, and it makes playing multiplayer online games with friends easy, but you can't use more than one Siri remote to play games on the same Apple TV at the same time. The Apple TV can only recognize one Siri Remote at a time, so if you want to play multiplayer games with someone else who's in your living room, you need third-party game controllers.

Managing In-App Purchases and Subscriptions

Many apps and games—especially ones that are free to download—offer ways for you to spend money after you're using them. These opportunities to spend come in two forms: subscriptions and in-app purchases.

Subscriptions are fairly straightforward: subscribe to Netflix for $8/month and you'll be billed every month until you cancel.

In-app purchases are a bit different (though if you've encountered them on the iPhone and iPad, you know what they are). They're one-time purchases you make in apps to improve your experience. For instance, a game might offer in-app purchases to give your character more in-game money to spend or to unlock a new set of levels, whereas a productivity app might add features or remove advertising after an in-app purchase.

In-app purchases are billed to the credit card on file in your Apple ID and, because it feels like you're barely buying anything at all, can add up quickly.

Make In-App Purchases

Every app that includes in-app purchases handles them a little differently, but the broad outlines of how to buy items in games roughly follow these steps (using Offroad Legends 2 as an example):

1. After you're in the game, look for options to upgrade, buy, or unlock. In this case, it's Unlock Cars. Select that option.

2. Find the thing you want to buy and select it.

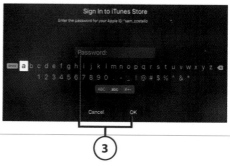

3. Log in to your Apple ID by entering your password and clicking OK.

4. The screen that appears specifies what you're buying and for how much. If you've changed your mind, select Cancel. To continue with the in-app purchase, select Buy.

5. The in-app purchase is complete, and the new item you bought is now available for you to use in the game.

Turn Off In-App Purchases

If you like to keep tight control of your budget—and especially if you have children in the house who might be tempted to buy things in apps without realizing the cost—you might prefer to disable all in-app purchases. This restricts your ability to buy things in some apps, but it will save you money, too.

To disable in-app purchases, follow these steps:

1. Launch Settings.

2. Select General.

3. Select Restrictions.

4. In the Parental Controls section, select the Restrictions menu to toggle it to On.

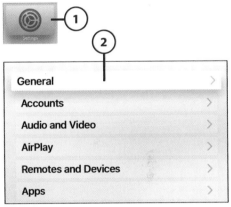

5. Set a four-digit passcode and then confirm it; this protects your Restrictions settings from being changed.

6. In the iTunes Store section, select In-App Purchases to toggle it to Block.

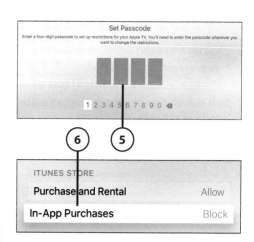

Re-enable In-App Purchases

To allow in-app purchases again, follow the first 4 steps in the preceding tutorial, with step 4 toggling Restrictions to Off, and enter your passcode when you're asked to do so.

Manage Your Subscriptions

If you've subscribed to anything on your Apple TV (or on your iOS device), and are billing that subscription to the credit card in your Apple ID, you can change or cancel that subscription on the Apple TV. The exact options depend on what's offered by the service—some allow you to upgrade to higher levels of service, others just have one and thus only let you cancel.

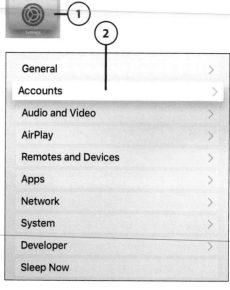

To change or cancel your subscriptions, follow these steps:

1. Launch Settings.

2. Select Accounts.

3. Select Manage Subscriptions.

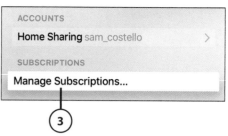

4. Sign in to your Apple ID.

5. On the screen that appears is a list of all the apps that you have paid subscriptions to. Select the app whose subscription you want to manage.

6. The screen that appears details what kind of subscription you have, how much it costs, and gives you the option to cancel it. In most cases, subscriptions are month-to-month and auto-matically renew (though some are annual). To cancel the subscription, select Turn Off Automatic Renewal.

7. Confirm your choice by selecting Turn Off.

Your subscription will continue through the end of its current period (for instance, for a monthly subscription, it continues through the end of the current month) and then cancels and you're no longer charged for it.

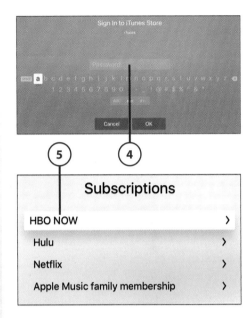

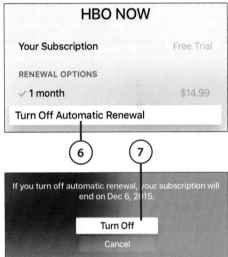

Updating Apps to New Versions

After you've installed some apps on your Apple TV, expect new versions of those apps to be released regularly. App updates fix bugs, add features, and make sure the app keeps working properly with new versions of the tvOS that runs the Apple TV.

Updating apps is almost always the right choice. Occasionally an update has a bug that causes problems, but developers usually fix those very quickly.

You can update your apps two ways: automatically or manually.

Enable Automatic App Updates

On the iPhone or iPad, allowing apps to automatically update means sacrificing battery life and potentially going over your monthly data limit (if you enable it to use cellular data for updates). The Apple TV doesn't have either of those restrictions, so setting it to automatically update its apps when new versions are available makes sense. Here's how:

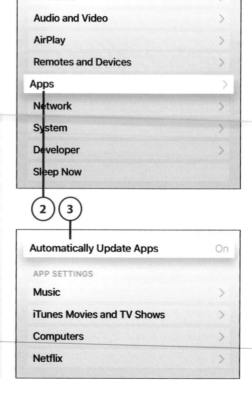

1. Launch Settings.

2. Select Apps.

3. Select the Automatically Update Apps menu to toggle it to On.

Now you can be sure you're always running the latest version of your apps, with all the features and bug fixes that come with them.

Apps Worth Checking Out

In an App Store of tens of thousands of apps (a number that will rise to hundreds of thousands quickly enough, if the iPhone App Store is any guide), narrowing down a list of recommendations to just a few apps is hard. That's why so many chapters of this book have specific app recommendations. Here are some apps—and games!—that don't quite fit in those chapters but that you should consider checking out.

Guitar Hero Live—A reinvention of the classic Guitar Hero game in which you play along with hits and rock your way to the top. Although you can use the Siri Remote with Guitar Hero Live, you'll have more fun if you buy the $99 guitar controller that lets you use an instrument while playing. The game includes hundreds of songs and access to GHTV, a live streaming video channel that you can play along with.

Madefire—Madefire brings comics and graphic novels to the Apple TV, but with a twist: These comics move. Called Motion Comics, the offerings here combine traditional comics with limited animation to bring the comic pages to vibrant life. Look for titles from big-name publishers such as DC Comics, Dark Horse, and IDW.

Galaxy on Fire: Manticore Rising —Take control of a space fighter plane in this science-fiction space battle game. Use the Siri Remote, or a game controller, to pilot your fighter through all kinds of space battles and marvel at the beautiful 3D graphics on display.

Air Wings—A new twist on the classic flying game. In this case, you're not piloting a normal plane, but instead are guiding a paper airplane through a room packed with treasure, weapons, and obstacles. Play on your own, against friends, or against players from around the world.

Podcasts by MyTuner—The Apple TV doesn't come with a built-in podcasts app, so Podcasts by MyTuner is a good option if you're looking to keep up to date on your favorite podcasts. It provides a store-style interface for finding audio and video podcasts, including some of the most popular series such as This American Life, Hardcore History, and Serial.

7 Minute Workout—Your Apple TV doesn't have to just be about sitting back on the couch and watching things passively. A bunch of apps can help you get active and stay fit, too. 7 Minute Workout is a good one for those of us pressed for time. As the name suggests, it provides a series of exercises and workouts that you can do in just seven minutes.

Forget all the movies, TV shows, and games. The Apple
TV also gives you access to tens of millions of songs.

Music isn't the first thing that comes to mind when you think about your TV, but with the Apple TV, making your TV the center of your home audio system is easy. In this chapter, you'll learn about:

→ Accessing and playing your music
→ Using Apple Music
→ Listening to music
→ Discovering new music in Apple Music
→ Tuning in radio on your TV
→ Using Pandora on Apple TV
→ Music apps to check out

6

Music Television: Music on the Apple TV

There are essentially two types of music that you can enjoy on the Apple TV: music that you own and music that you rent.

- **Music that you own** is music you've bought from the iTunes Store and other online stores or copied from CDs. After you've paid for this music once, you own it and can do with it what you want. This music gets to your Apple TV via iCloud and the pre-installed Music app or Home Sharing.

- **Music that you rent** is music that you access using streaming services such as Apple Music or Pandora. You pay a monthly subscription for this music and lose it when you cancel. This music gets to your Apple TV through the Music app with Apple Music enabled or through third-party apps you download from the App Store.

The type of music best for you depends on many factors, but the key one is your level of comfort with renting music. It seems strange at first, but getting unlimited access to the tens of millions of songs in iTunes for the cost of one album each month is pretty compelling. The question really is, "How much does being tied to a monthly subscription to maintain access to the music bother you?" If the answer is "Not much," Apple Music, Pandora, and similar services are great options.

Of course, you don't have to pick one or the other. You can use both options together for a complete experience.

Accessing and Playing Your Music

If you want to enjoy only music that you own, you have two options: the music stored in your iCloud account or the music on your computer, accessed using Home Sharing. Both work fine, and can work together, but which you prefer probably depends on how much of your music is in the cloud.

Access Your iTunes Music Library

All the music you've ever bought from iTunes is available on your Apple TV through iCloud for no extra cost (music you've gotten from other sources and added to iCloud using iTunes Match is also available here). Just find the music you want, play it, and the song streams right to your Apple TV. Here's how:

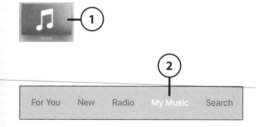

1. Launch the Music app.

2. Use the remote to select the My Music menu at the top of the TV screen.

3. The first time you do this, you're asked to Turn on iCloud Music Library. Apple uses this tool to connect music libraries across Macs, PCs, iOS devices, and the Apple TV. Select Turn on iCloud Music Library using the touchpad.

4. A bar moves across the screen to indicate the progress of turning on iCloud Music Library and downloading information about all of your iTunes purchases.

5. When that's done, the My Music menu appears on the right side of the screen, which lets you shuffle songs or view them by Artist, Album, Song, Genre, and more.

You need to be logged in to your Apple ID to access iCloud Music Library. You should have logged in when you set up the Apple TV, but if you didn't, go to Settings -> Accounts -> iCloud and sign in.

>>>Go Further

USE ITUNES MATCH TO PUT ALL YOUR MUSIC IN THE CLOUD

The music you've bought from iTunes might be only a small percentage of your total music library. If that's the case, accessing only your iTunes purchases might leave you with just a few tunes. One solution to this is to sign up for iTunes Match.

iTunes Match is a $25/year Apple service that takes *all* the music in your iTunes library—not just what you've bought from iTunes—and adds it to your iCloud account. As long as you keep the subscription, your entire music library stays in that account and available on your Apple TV (and iOS device and computer).

It's both a great backup of your music and a good way to get all your music to your Apple TV if you don't use Apple Music.

To learn more about iTunes Match and to sign up for it, go to http://www.apple.com/itunes/itunes-match/ in a web browser.

Use Your Full iTunes Library on the Apple TV

The iCloud Music Library contains only music you bought from iTunes or added using iTunes Match. If you have a lot of music in your iTunes library that you got in other ways—from CDs, friends, or other music stores—it won't show up in iCloud. Use Home Sharing to access that music on the Apple TV. Follow these steps to access your music via Home Sharing:

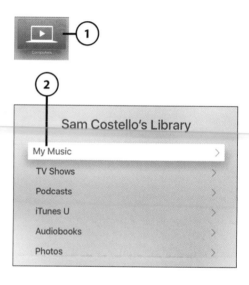

1. Launch Computers.

2. With Home Sharing turned on, a list of the kinds of content you can access from your computer appears. Select My Music.

Turning On Home Sharing

To use Home Sharing, you need to have it turned it on, have the computer you want to share with turned on, and have iTunes open. If you haven't turned on Home Sharing, check out "Enable Home Sharing" in Chapter 3, "Using iTunes for TV and Movies."

---

3. Browse or search the iTunes library stored on your computer. For more details on how to do that, check out the next two tutorials.

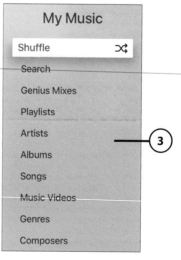

Browse Your Music Library

After your music library is available on the Apple TV using either iCloud Music Library or Home Sharing, browse it to find the music you want to listen to. Here's how:

1. Launch Music.

2. Use the remote to highlight and select My Music.

3. The menu on the right contains categories that you can browse: Recently Added (only visible if you subscribe to Apple Music), Artists, Albums, Songs, Genres, Composers, and so on. Use the remote to highlight one and select it by clicking the touchpad.

4. If you select Recently Added, this screen displays a list of all the albums you've added to your library from Apple Music recently. The list is ordered from most recently added to oldest. Select an album to view or play its songs.

5. If you select Artists in step 3, all artists in your music library display in alphabetical order. Select an artist to see all albums by that artist in your library.

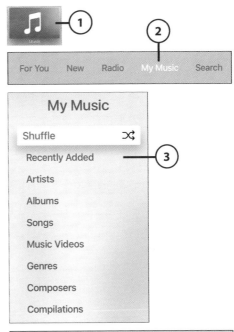

6. Select one of the albums to see all songs on that album or the All Songs menu to see every song by that artist in a single list.

7. If you select Albums in step 3, all the albums in your music library display in alphabetical order. Select an album to see all the songs it contains.

8. If you select Songs in step 3, every song in your music library displays in alphabetical order, without regard to artist or album. Select a song to start playing it.

9. If you select Genre in step 3, the genres that your artists/albums are from display in alphabetical order. Select a genre to see all artists from that genre.

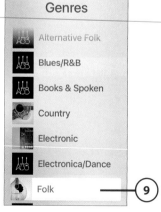

Search Your Music Library

Browsing isn't your only option for finding music; you can search, too. If you know exactly what you're looking for, follow these steps:

1. Launch Music.

2. Use the remote to highlight and select Search in the top menu.

3. Type in the name of the song, artist, album, and so on that you're looking for using the onscreen keyboard or the Remote app.

4. Suggested matches display toward the bottom of the screen as you type.

5. When you're done entering your search or see what you want in the suggested matches, swipe down on the remote.

6. The Music app displays results that match your search.

7. The two options for filtering search results are All Apple Music and My Music.

8. Select the All Apple Music toggle to see all the matches for your search that exist in Apple Music.

9. Select My Music to see search results that exist only in your iCloud Music Library or iTunes library.

In either view, use the remote to navigate around the screen. Selecting an artist or album shows more content about that selection. Selecting a song starts it playing.

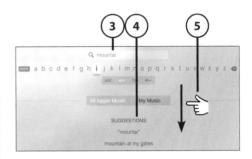

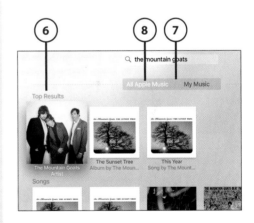

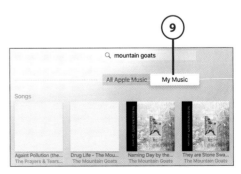

Use Siri to Search for Music

Just like Siri can help you find movies and TV shows to watch, it can also help you find music to listen to. If you have music in your iCloud Music Library, Siri can search that. But if you subscribe to Apple Music, it searches that library and the whole, seemingly endless, Apple Music catalog. Use Siri to search for music by following these steps:

1. Hold down the microphone button on the remote control to activate Siri.

2. Speak your search. For example, "find the album *The Pinkprint* by Nicki Minaj" or "Show me songs by Nirvana."

Siri's Limitations

As of this writing, Siri isn't able to search for specific songs, just albums and artists. Expect that to change as Apple improves Siri on the TV. In fact, by the time you read this, that feature might already be available.

3. If you searched for an album, you should go directly to that album's detail screen, where you can play songs, add it to your library, favorite it, and more.

4. If you searched for an artist, you'll see a screen featuring all kinds of content by that artist: most popular songs, top albums, videos, a full listing of albums, and the option to create a radio station based on the artist. (For more on custom radio stations, check out "Create Custom Radio Stations" later in this chapter.)

5. Use the remote to navigate to the content you want and click the touchpad to select it. Selecting a song or video starts it playing. Selecting an album takes you to the album detail screen.

Using Apple Music

If you've ever dreamed about having unlimited access to virtually every song and every album by any artist, I have good news for you: You can get it for just $10/month with Apple Music ($15 for a Family subscription). Though a handful of notable exceptions exist, Apple Music lets you stream practically every one of the 30 million songs in the iTunes Store to any compatible device. This section helps you use it if you're already a subscriber or want to give it a try.

An Apple Music Subscription Works on All Your Apple Devices

One great feature of Apple Music is that it's not limited just to the Apple TV. No matter what device you use to subscribe, you can use Apple Music on all other compatible devices. So, if you sign up here, you can also use it on your iPhone and in iTunes on your computer. That's a pretty good deal.

Sign Up for Apple Music

If you're even remotely interested in Apple Music, you should sign up. The service offers a 90-day free trial so you can subscribe, check it out, and cancel without paying anything if you don't like it or prefer a different streaming solution, such as Spotify. There's no downside to that (except forgetting to cancel!).

You can't sign up for Apple Music on the Apple TV, so I'm not going to provide a full tutorial here. If you want a step-by-step tutorial on how to sign up, check out my article on the topic at http://ipod.about.com/od/gettingmusicforyouripod/ss/How-to-Sign-Up-for-Apple-Music.htm.

After you've signed up, as long as your subscription is active, Apple will bill $9.99 each month to the credit or debit card on file in your Apple ID.

If more than one person in your household wants to use Apple Music, consider signing up for a Family Plan. These provide all the benefits of Apple Music for up to 6 people—for only $14.99 a month. That's just $5 extra for 5 more users.

It's Not All Good

Forget to Cancel and You'll Pay

Whether you're coming to the end of your free trial or cancelling a standard subscription, make sure you do it before the last day of the month. If you don't cancel in time and the next billing period—that is, the next month—starts, you'll have to pay for the next month's worth of service. This is especially annoying if you forget to cancel your free trial and end up spending money when you had intended to not pay anything. Don't expect to be able to appeal or get any refunds from Apple on this one.

Cancel Apple Music

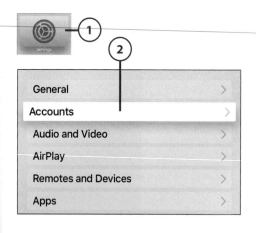

You might not be able to sign up for Apple Music on the Apple TV, but you can cancel your subscription. If you've tried it out and decided that Apple Music isn't for you, cancel your subscription by following these steps:

1. Launch Settings.

2. Select Accounts.

3. Select Manage Subscriptions. (At this point, you might be asked to log in to your Apple ID. If so, log in.)

4. Select Apple Music (depending on your subscription, it should read individual or family membership).

5. Select Turn Off Automatic Renewal.

6. If you change your mind and want to continue your Apple Music subscription, select Cancel. To confirm the cancellation, select Turn Off.

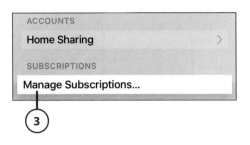

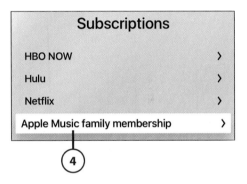

Add Songs and Albums from Apple Music to Your Library

After you've found a song or album in Apple Music, save it to your library so that it's always easy to enjoy. Apple Music mixes music from the service with your personal music library so you can find all your music in one location. Follow these steps to add items from Apple Music to your library:

1. Search Apple Music and find and select a song or album you want to add to your library.

2. **To add an album:** On the screen that displays all the songs on an album, highlight the Add button just beneath the album art and select it.

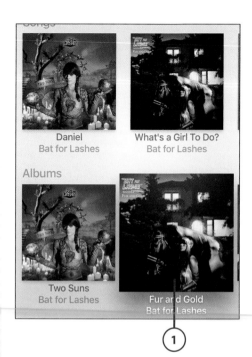

3. **To add a song:** Start playing the song. When the song is playing, click the touchpad to reveal the three-dot button at the top of the screen. Select the three-dot button.

4. Select Add to My Music.

>>>Go Further
ADD SONGS AND ALBUMS WITH SIRI

Siri can help you add songs to your music library. When you're listening to a song you like, just hold down the mic button on the remote control and say "add this song to my library" or "add this album to my music."

Remove Apple Music Songs or Albums from Your Library

After adding a song or album from Apple Music to your library you might decide you don't like it and want to get rid of it. To delete an Apple Music item from your library (this only works with items from Apple Music, not from your iCloud Music Library), follow these steps:

1. Find and select the item you want to remove. You can do this by searching for it using the Search menu or by browsing. To browse, highlight My Music and then select Artists, Albums, or Songs on the right-hand side.

Removing a Song

If you want to remove a single song, rather than a full album, start playing the song and skip to step 4.

2. Items that are in your music library display the In My Music button. Highlight and select it.

3. If you change your mind, select Cancel. Otherwise, select Remove from My Music.

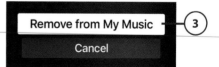

4. When the song is playing, click the touchpad to reveal and select the three-dot button at the top of the screen.

5. Select Remove from My Music.

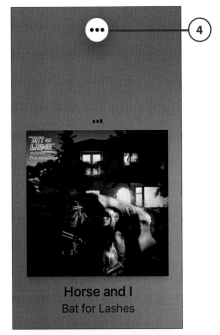

It's Not All Good

It's Not All Good: You Can't Remove a Song With Siri

Believe it or not, you can't remove a song from your music library with Siri. That's right: Although Siri may be able to add a song to your library, it can't take one away. Expect Apple to add that feature in the future.

Listening to Music

Finding music and adding it to your library is all well and good, but all of that has just one goal: listening to the music. Playing music through your sound-bar or home theater system can make for a great listening experience and the Music app offers a set of powerful features. Whether you're just listening to your own music or combining your music with what you find at Apple Music, these instructions will help you enjoy your tunes.

Play Your Music

The exact steps required to play music depend on what screen you start at. For the purposes of this tutorial, we'll assume that you searched or browsed to find an artist using the Music app. If you started with an album or song, skip the appropriate steps at the beginning of the tutorial:

1. Select the artist whose music you want to play and click the touch-pad.

2. In the list of the artist's albums, select the album you want to listen to and click the touchpad.

3. From the listing of songs on this album, select the song you want to listen to and click the touch-pad. To listen to the whole album, click the first song and let it play.

>>>Go Further

SIRI CAN PLAY MUSIC, TOO

Siri makes it easy for you to play music. Just hold down the Siri button on the remote control and say things like:

- "Play Adele" to hear a randomly selected mix of popular songs by the British songstress.

- "Play No Depression by Uncle Tupelo" to hear that Americana song.

- "Play the Album I Want to See the Bright Lights Tonight" to begin listening to that album.

- "Play My Top Rated Playlist" (or the name of any other playlist you have) to start listening to the playlist you named. Remember: Unless you have Apple Music, you'll get errors if you search for something you don't have in your music library.

Master the Playback Screen

When music is playing on your Apple TV, the playback screen contains these options:

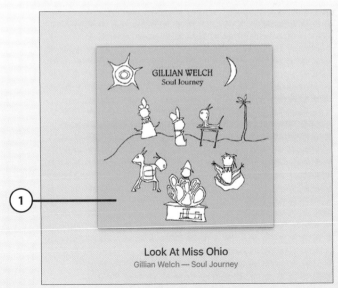

1. There are no controls on the default playback screen. The music responds to the Play/Pause button on the remote, of course, but it can also respond to other actions.

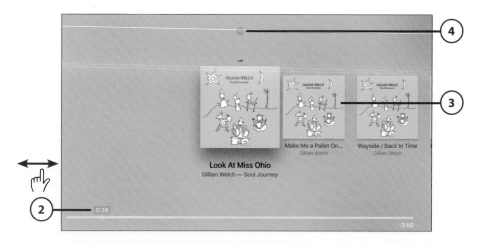

2. Click the touchpad to reveal a progress bar for the song. Move forward and backward in the song by swiping sideways on the touchpad.

3. When you do this, the other songs on the album are also revealed. Swipe side to side to jump to other songs. Click the touchpad to play the song you've highlighted.

4. When the progress bar and list of songs appear on the screen, a small, round button with three dots in it also appears at the top of the screen. Select it to explore other options.

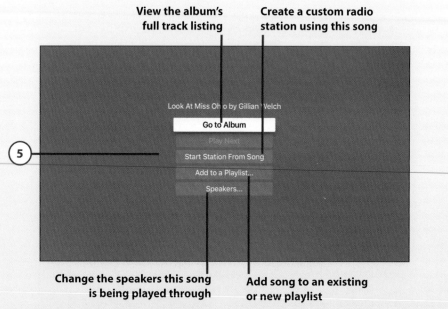

5. The options you see on this screen vary depending on a number of factors: whether the music is in your library, whether you have favorited it, and so on. These options are for a song you own as part of your iTunes library.

Tell Apple Music to give you more songs like this one

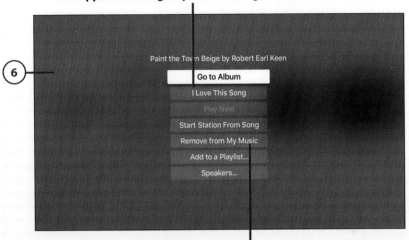

Paint the Town Beige by Robert Earl Keen

Go to Album

I Love This Song

Play Next

Start Station From Song

Remove from My Music

Add to a Playlist...

Speakers...

This song is in your Apple Music library; remove it

6. Another version of that screen appears with options for a song you got from Apple Music.

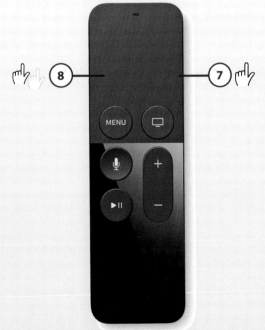

7. To skip to the next track while you listen to music, click the right side of the touchpad once.

8. To skip back to the previous track while listening, click the left side of the touchpad twice.

Siri Works Here, Too

You can also use Siri to skip to the next or previous song by saying "play the next song" or "play the previous song."

Favorite Songs

There's a good reason to share information about your musical taste with Apple Music: It can help you discover new music. When you're listening to a song, you can "favorite" a song, which tells Apple Music you really like it. The service then uses that information to better customize its recommendations for you.

You can favorite songs by doing the following:

1. Start playing the song you want to favorite.

2. Click the touchpad on the remote to reveal and select the three-dot button at the top of the screen.

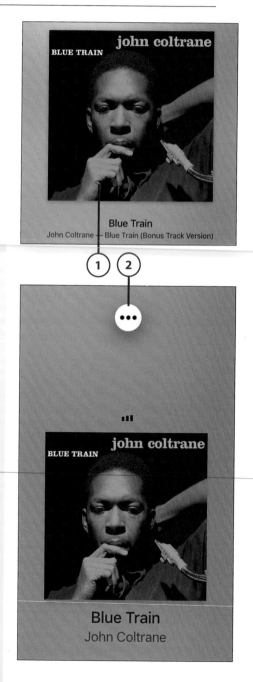

3. Select I Love This Song.

You can also favorite entire albums. Just go to the album screen and select the Love button just below the album art.

Get Recommendations

For more on getting these recommendations, check out "Get Recommendations from Apple For You," later in this chapter.

Shuffle Your Music

Listening to a random sampling of your music library is a great way to rediscover songs, get out of a music rut, or simply put music on and not think about it again. Here's what you need to do to shuffle your music library:

1. Launch Music.

2. Use the remote to highlight and select the My Music menu.

3. At this point, you have to choose what kind of shuffle you want. To shuffle within a single artist, skip to step 5. To shuffle within a single album, skip to step 9. To shuffle among every song in your Music app, highlight and select the Shuffle menu on this screen.

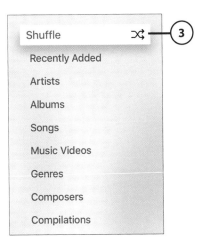

4. When the music is playing, click the touchpad once to see what songs are coming up. Use the instructions in "Master the Playback Screen" earlier in this chapter to learn how to skip forward and backward, and the other options you have here.

5. To shuffle all songs in your library by a single artist, return to My Music and select the Artists menu.

6. Navigate to the artist and select him or her.

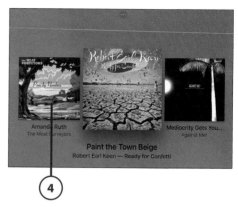

④

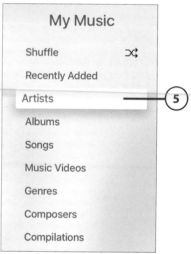

⑤

⑥

7. Select All Songs.

8. Select Shuffle.

9. To shuffle the songs within a single album only, return to My Music and select the Albums menu.

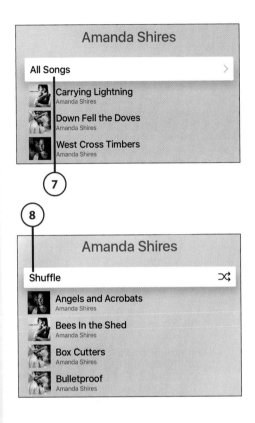

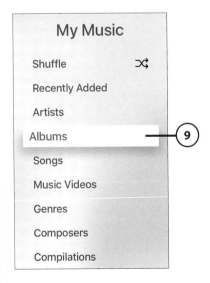

10. Navigate to the album you want to shuffle and select it.

11. Select Shuffle.

Siri Shuffles

It probably won't surprise you to learn that Siri can perform all the shuffle commands detailed in the last tutorial. Just activate Siri and you can say something like "shuffle songs by Robert Earl Keen" or "shuffle the album The Harrow & The Harvest."

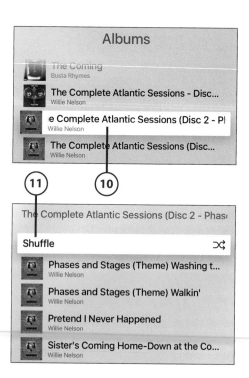

Use Playlists

Playlists are a fun way to create mixes for different seasons, moods, or tasks. Any playlists you create with iTunes or using the Music app for your iPhone or iPad are also available to you in Apple TV. Here's what you need to do to use them:

1. Launch the Music app.

2. At the top of the screen, use the remote to highlight and select the Playlists menu.

3. The screen that appears displays all the playlists available in your iCloud Music Library account. Use the remote to navigate to and select one you're interested in.

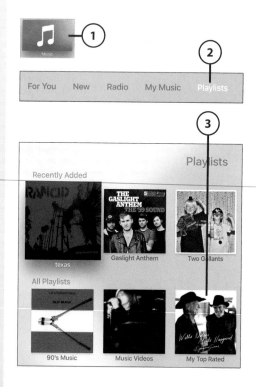

4. To listen to the playlist all the way through, select the first song. You can also swipe up and down through the playlist to find individual songs.

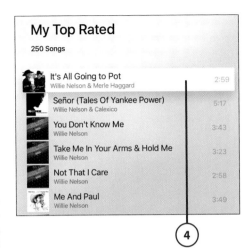

My Top Rated

250 Songs

It's All Going to Pot Willie Nelson & Merle Haggard		2:59
Señor (Tales Of Yankee Power) Willie Nelson & Calexico		5:17
You Don't Know Me Willie Nelson		3:43
Take Me In Your Arms & Hold Me Willie Nelson		3:23
Not That I Care Willie Nelson		2:58
Me And Paul Willie Nelson		3:49

It's Not All Good

Create a Playlist in Apple TV

Although you *can* create playlists on the Apple TV, it's a cumbersome and frustrating process. To save both space, your sanity, and mine, I've skipped tutorials on that subject and instead suggest that if you want to use playlists on your Apple TV, you create them on a computer in iTunes or on a mobile device. If you do that and have iCloud Music Library enabled on the device where you created the playlist, your playlists are available on the Apple TV automatically.

Use Sound Check to Equalize Song Volumes

Different albums are recorded at different volume levels (generally speaking, older albums are quieter, but that's not an ironclad rule). That's fine when you're just listening to the album, but if you're shuffling songs or listening to a playlist, each song changing volume is annoying and disruptive. The Music app can solve this for you with a feature called Sound Check.

Sound Check automatically adjusts the volume of the songs you're listening to so that they're all basically even. Turn it on by following these steps:

1. Launch Settings.

2. Select Apps.

3. In the App Settings section, select Music.

4. Select the Sound Check menu to toggle it to On.

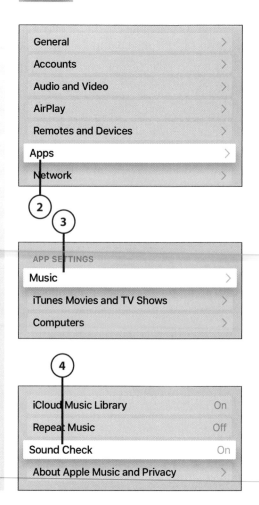

Discover New Music in Apple Music

As you've seen so far, the Music app makes it easy to find and enjoy your music. But that's all music from artists you already know. What about ones you haven't discovered yet? One of the best features of Apple Music is that it gets to know your taste and introduces you to new musicians you'll love.

Get Recommendations from Apple with For You

Unlike other services that do this using algorithms (a method that has merits), Apple opted for hired experts in all genres of music to help you find new artists based on your taste. It does that through the For You section of the Music app.

For You takes the data Apple has about the music you like, compares it with other people who use the service, and then involves experts in the styles you like to curate a selection of music recommendations for you. You'll get recommendations for albums as well as customized playlists that focus on different artists and themes.

To access the For You content:

1. Launch Music.

2. Use the remote to highlight and select the For You menu.

3. For You delivers two kinds of recommendations: playlists and albums. Playlists are themed around specific topics and artists that Apple Music's curators think you'll enjoy based on your taste. Albums are just what they sound like: albums that other people like you enjoy.

4. Use the remote to browse the recommendations. When you find one that looks interesting, click the touchpad to see more about it.

On the detail screen of either the album or playlist, you can listen to and control songs using the techniques described earlier in this chapter.

A recommended album

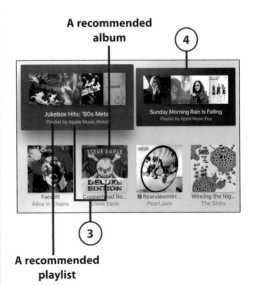

A recommended playlist

Improve the For You Recommendations

The first few times you use it, For You might not seem incredibly helpful. In fact, it might not seem to know you very well at all. But the more you use Apple Music, and the more information you give it about your taste, the better its suggestions get. That's because it builds its understanding of who you are and what you like over time based on your behavior.

Although just using the Music app gives it some data, you can do two things to really improve your For You recommendations:

- **Favorite Songs**—As noted earlier in the chapter, using the I Love This Song or Album button tells Apple Music that this is something you really like. The more music you love, the better Apple Music will know your taste.

- **Reject Recommendations**—Even though you can favorite songs and albums on the Apple TV, you can't reject For You recommendations. Why Apple left this feature out I don't know; perhaps it will show up in future versions of the operating system. In the meantime, you can reject recommendations to improve your results in iTunes or on your mobile device.

Check Out the Latest Releases

Besides recommending content for you, Apple Music also features a section of recent releases called New. On that screen, you'll find hot new albums, popular singles, music videos, new playlists, and more. Use the New screen this way:

1. Launch Music.

2. Use the remote to highlight and select New.

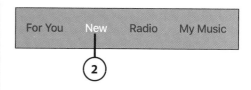

3. On the New screen, content is broken up into sections such as feature releases, Hot Tracks, playlists, new albums, music videos, and more.

4. Use the remote to navigate the screen. When you find something you want to listen to highlight your selection and click the touchpad.

If you select a song or music video, it plays right away. If you choose an album or playlist, the track listing displays. Either way, use the commands from earlier in the chapter to control playback.

Tuning In Radio on Your TV

Apple Music isn't just a virtually infinite jukebox; it also offers new kinds of radio stations. From stations that mimic traditional radio to stations curated by experts to stations you create yourself based on your preferences, Apple Music makes it easy to get the radio experience streamed over the Internet into your living room.

The headline station for Apple's radio services is Beats 1. Broadcast out of studios in New York, London, and Los Angeles, Beats 1 offers 12 hours a day of music that sounds better than anything you'll hear on an FM dial these days. (It's 12 hours a day for one half of the world, and those 12 hours of programming are replayed in other time zones around the world to give Beats 1 full 24-hour coverage.) It's run by big-name DJs Zane Low, Ebro Darden, and Julie Adenuga, and features regular guest shows by artists such as Drake, Q-Tip, and Elton John. With all that musical talent and knowledge on hand, you can be sure that you'll hear a wider variety and better mix of songs, as well as great interviews and commentary.

The Beats 1 Show Schedule

To check out the schedule of what DJs and shows are coming up on Beats 1 this month, visit http://applemusic.tumblr.com.

Listen to Beats 1

Although Beats 1 is one of the headline features of Apple Music, it's
actually available to anyone with an
Apple TV (or iOS device or computer
running iTunes), even if you don't
subscribe to the service. Here's what
you need to do to listen to Beats 1:

Use Siri Instead

You can skip this entire tutorial by
telling Siri, "Play Beats 1." The radio
station will start right up.

1. Launch Music.

2. Use the remote to highlight and
    select Radio.

3. Highlight the Beats 1 banner at
    the top of the screen (you'll know
    you've done this when the Listen
    Now button turns white).

4. Select the Listen Now button to
    start playing Beats 1 radio.

5. The playback screen displays the
    song and artist being played. The
    three-dot button is available at
    the top of the screen to add a
    song to your library or favorite it.

Gratitude with Bomba Estereo
Beats 1

>>>Go Further

HOW TO REQUEST SONGS ON BEATS 1

Beats 1 might be a modern Internet radio station, but it has a feature familiar to anyone who's listened to radio for the last half-century or more: song requests. You can vote for what you would like to hear on Beats 1 and it might get on the air. To request a song from within the United States, call 1-877-720-6293. If you're in another country, check out http://applemusic.tumblr.com/requests for the phone number in your country.

Enjoy Curated Radio Stations in Your Favorite Genres

Beats 1 isn't the only kind of radio available on the Apple TV. You can also enjoy radio stations created and curated by Apple's team of music experts in all kinds of genres. These stations aren't quite as dynamic as Beats 1—they don't change content every day, they don't have hosts and shows, etc.—but if you're looking for a long-form playlist of songs in a particular genre or influence, they're a great choice.

Curated radio stations are available whether or not you have an Apple Music subscription. Here's how to use them:

1. Launch Music.

2. Use the remote to highlight and select Radio.

3. Use the remote control to browse the stations and select one that interests you.

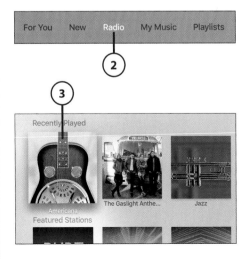

4. Just like when listening to a playlist or shuffling, a song appears onscreen and starts to play.

5. To see the songs you've listened to, or to add a song to your library or favorite it, click the touchpad and select the three-dot button at the top of the screen.

6. On the screen that appears, select a button to favorite the song, start a custom radio station from it, add it to your music library, and more.

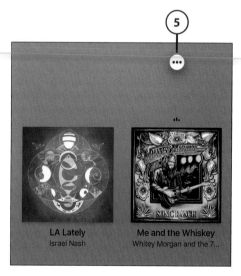

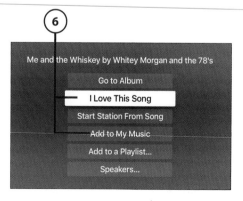

It's Not All Good

Hate Ads? Subscribe to Apple Music

If you don't have Apple Music, the curated radio stations play ads every few songs. If you want to avoid ads, you need to subscribe to Apple Music.

>>>Go Further

SKIPPING SONGS

Unlike on Beats 1, in curated radio stations, you can skip songs you don't like. Beats 1 is essentially live, so there's no way to skip into the future, but because curated stations are pre-programmed you can move around all you like. Strangely, you can only skip songs when the full album art is onscreen, not when the three-dot button or the list of songs played is present. When the album art is taking up the whole screen, click the right side of the remote's touchpad to skip forward. If you have a subscription, you can skip an unlimited number of songs. If you don't, you'll only be able to skip six songs every hour.

Create Custom Radio Stations

If Beats 1 and the curated radio stations inspire you, you can create your own custom radio stations in Music. If you've used Pandora, the concept is very similar: start a station based on an artist or song and you'll hear related songs. Provide feedback around what you like and dislike to tune the station to your taste.

To create your own custom radio station, follow these steps:

1. Begin by finding a song you want to use as the foundation of your custom radio station and play it.

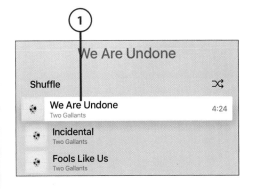

2. When the song is playing click the touchpad to reveal and select the three-dot icon at the top of the screen.

3. Select Start Station From Song.

4. A new song, similar or related to the first song, starts playing. Future songs will be related, but randomly selected.

If you like the custom station you've created and want to listen to it again, just go to the main screen of the Radio section of the app and look for it in the Recently Played section.

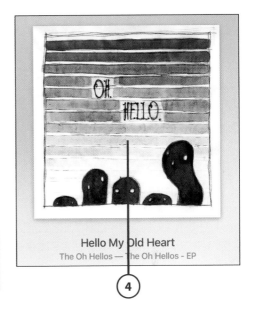

Hello My Old Heart
The Oh Hellos — The Oh Hellos - EP

④

It's Not All Good

Skip Limits Still Apply

As mentioned earlier in the chapter, if you don't have an Apple Music subscription, you can only skip six songs an hour on curated radio stations. The same six-skip limit applies to radio stations you create for yourself.

Modify Your Curated or Custom Radio Stations

After you've created a radio station, you can perfect it by telling Apple Music what songs you like and dislike (again, this is just like Pandora). Here's how:

1. Start listening to a curated or custom radio station. It can be an existing station or a new one.

Hello My Old Heart
The Oh Hellos — The Oh Hellos - EP

①

2. Click the touchpad to reveal and select the three-dot button at the top of the screen.

3. What options you see on the screen that appears depend on what kind of station you're listening to. On curated stations, you can favorite the song, as covered earlier. On custom stations, though, you have more flexibility. If you like the song and want to hear more like it on this station in the future, select Play More Like This. If don't want to hear this song—or similar ones—again, select Never Play This Song.

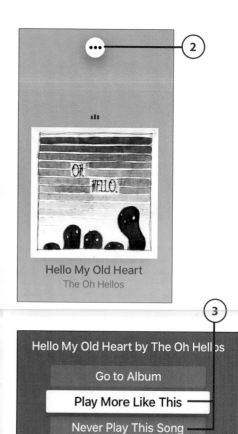

Hello My Old Heart
The Oh Hellos

Hello My Old Heart by The Oh Hellos

Go to Album

Play More Like This

Never Play This Song

Start Station From Song

Add to My Music

Add to a Playlist...

Speakers...

It's Not All Good

You Can't Delete Custom Radio Stations on Apple TV

For whatever reason, Apple has not provided a feature on the Apple TV that allows you to delete any custom radio stations you've created from the TV itself. Instead, if you want to get rid of any stations, you'll need to use iTunes or your mobile device.

>>>*Go Further*

USING PODCASTS AND AUDIOBOOKS ON APPLE TV

If you're an enthusiast of non-music audio content such as podcasts and audio books, you might have noticed there are no built-in apps to handle them. But that doesn't mean you can't use them. Turn on Home Sharing and, if you have any available in the iTunes library being shared, you can access them using the Computers app. Check out "Use Your Full iTunes Library on the Apple TV" earlier in the chapter for more details.

Using Pandora on Apple TV

Pandora is one of the most widely used music streaming services on the Internet. If you're a Pandora fan and an Apple TV owner, there's good news: There's a Pandora app.

You can't create an account using the Pandora app right now, but if you have an account, you can log into it and enjoy all your stations. While you're playing stations, you can give songs a thumbs up or thumbs down, or skip songs.

Even better, you can create new stations using the app, too. Choose from suggested stations or search for an artist, song, or genre to use as the starting point of the new station.

You can even delete stations: Just select the station you want to delete and hold down the touchpad on the remote until the Delete button appears. Select that button, and the station is removed from your Pandora account.

As of this writing, there are a few familiar Pandora features you can't use, such as sharing songs on social media, buying songs, reviewing all the songs you've ever liked, or following other users. Maybe those features will arrive in a future version, but for now, it's great to be able to enjoy all of your carefully curated Pandora stations on your home entertainment system.

Music Apps to Check Out

Music is the only music app that comes pre-installed on the Apple TV, but it's far from the only one you should check out. Just like on the iPhone, many interesting music apps exist—even some that compete with Apple Music. Here are a few worth a listen:

Receiver—If you prefer traditional, terrestrial radio to the stations Apple Music offers, you should check out Receiver. It lets you tune in the Internet streams of more than 22,000 broadcast radio stations from around the world. Search for stations by genre, language, or location; browse popular stations; and save your favorites for easy access later. **$0.99**

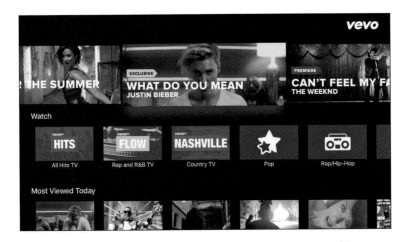

Vevo—Enjoying music isn't just about listening; it's also about watching. At least that's the case with the music video–centric app Vevo. Vevo offers videos from virtually every genre of music, along with original shows and live performances—all of which look great on your television in HD. Create playlists of your favorite videos, too. **Free**

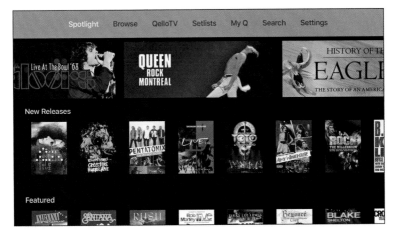

Qello—Get that live concert experience from the comfort of your living room with Qello, a service that delivers new and classic concerts, as well as music documentaries. The app boasts more than 1,500 performances from all sorts of bands, including major names such as Metallica, Lady Gaga, Beyoncé, Nirvana, Gary Clark Jr., and more. The app itself is free and offers a seven-day free trial. After that, you must subscribe. **$7.99/month**

At the time of this writing, the biggest player in streaming music, Spotify, does not have an app available for Apple TV. If you're interested in seeing that app, or similar ones, you should periodically check the App Store.

>>>Go Further
USE AIRPLAY FOR MUSIC APPS THAT AREN'T ON APPLE TV

Spotify and other streaming music apps might not be on the Apple TV yet, but you can still use them. If you listen to them on a device that supports AirPlay—like an iPhone, iPad, or Mac—you can send music from the device to the Apple TV to play on the TV's speakers or home theater system. For more on AirPlay and how to use it, check out "Using AirPlay and AirPlay Mirroring" in Chapter 7, "Advanced TV Topics."

**Turn your TV into a slideshow
with the Photos app**

All the features and functions of the Apple TV covered so far might seem like more than enough for one device, but this device can do many more things. In this chapter, you'll learn about advanced topics like:

7

→ Viewing photos and videos on your Apple TV

→ Customizing your home screen layout

→ Using content restrictions

→ Using AirPlay and AirPlay Mirroring

→ Understanding the Apple TV's advanced audio and video settings

Advanced TV Topics

After you know how to use the features covered in this chapter, you'll be able to use content stored on other devices on your Apple TV, fine-tune its AV output, and even restrict kids from accessing mature material.

Viewing Photos and Videos on Your Apple TV

The Apple TV is great for watching professionally produced movies and TV; it's also a terrific way to enjoy your home movies or still photographs.

Perhaps the simplest way to do this is by using Apple's iCloud online service. Among iCloud's many facets is a photos feature that allows iPhone and iPad users to upload the photos and videos they take with their mobile devices to the cloud. This feature, called iCloud Photos, can be configured to automatically or manually receive uploads. In fact, if you use an Apple device, you might already be using iCloud Photos.

Whether you're already using it or turn it on here, you'll need to add some photos and videos to your iCloud Photos library for them to show up on your Apple TV. If no photos are in your library, the Apple TV photos app will be blank.

>>>*Go Further*

ENABLE PHOTO STREAM ON IPHONE/IPAD AND MAC

To automatically upload all the photos and videos you take on your iPhone or iPad to iCloud, go to Settings, Photos & Cameras and move the My Photo Stream slider to On (green).

Do the same thing on a Mac by going to Apple menu, System Preferences, iCloud. Check the box next to Photos and check the boxes next to My Photo Stream and iCloud Photo Sharing.

Sign In to iCloud Photo Stream

If you upload your digital photos and videos to your iCloud Photo Stream account, you can enjoy them on your Apple TV using the pre-installed Photos app. To do that, you must first sign in to your account by following these steps:

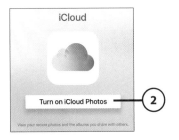

1. Launch Photos.

2. Highlight and select the Turn on iCloud Photos button.

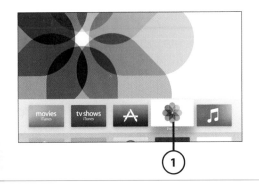

3. If you've already added photos to your iCloud Photos library, wait a few seconds and those albums and photos appear on your Apple TV.

View Photos and Videos on Your Apple TV

After you sign in to your iCloud account, viewing your photos and videos is simple. Here's what you need to do:

1. Launch Photos.

2. The Photos app displays whatever photo albums you've set up on your iOS device, on your Mac, or in iCloud. Use the remote to highlight and select the album you want to view.

3. All photos in the selected photo album display. Use the remote to navigate through the photos. When you find a photo you want to view at full size, highlight and click the photo using the touch-pad.

4. The photo displays at full-screen size. To move through other photos in the album swipe left or right. Swipe up to see more information about a photo or to like it.

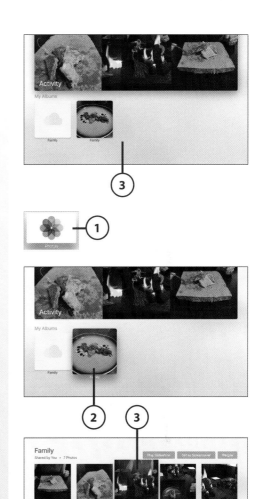

Use Apple TV to Display a Slideshow

Showing off photos from a recent vacation used to require slides and a projector. These days it just takes the Slideshow feature in the Photos app. Follow these steps to display a slideshow of your photos on the big screen using your Apple TV:

1. Launch Photos.

2. Use the touchpad to highlight and select the photo album whose photos you want to display as a slideshow.

3. On the photo album page, use the remote to highlight Play Slideshow and select it.

4. Before your photos start displaying, choose some slideshow settings or skip the settings by tapping Start Slideshow.

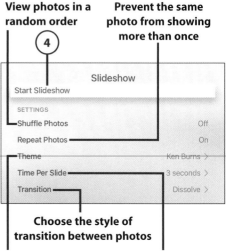

View photos in a random order

Prevent the same photo from showing more than once

Choose the style of transition between photos

Select a theme that applies effects and visual styles to your photos

Control how long each photo is shown

5. When your slideshow is playing, any settings you chose in step 4 apply. Click the touchpad to pause the slideshow or press the Menu button to quit.

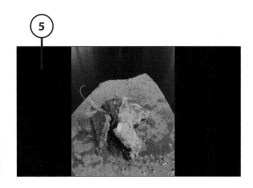

>>>Go Further

USE YOUR OWN PHOTOS AS SCREENSAVERS

The Apple TV comes with some beautiful photos and high-def videos to use as screensavers, but if you prefer to display your own photos, you can. Check out "Use Your Photos as Screensavers" in Chapter 8, "Take Control of Your Apple TV's Settings" for instructions on how to do that.

Access Photos on Your Computer Without Using iCloud

What if you don't upload your photos to iCloud? What if you manage your photos in a program on your computer? You can still view your photos and videos on your Apple TV; you just have to use Home Sharing:

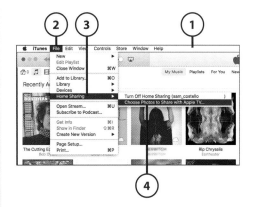

1. On your computer, open iTunes.

2. Click the File menu.

3. Click Home Sharing.

4. Click Choose Photos to Share with Apple TV.

Enable Home Sharing

For instructions on how to set up Home Sharing, check out "How to Enable Home Sharing" in Chapter 3, "Using iTunes for TV and Movies."

5. In the Photo Sharing Preferences window that pops up, check the box next to Share Photos from.

6. Choose whether you want to share all of your photos (the default) or select the photo albums you want to share. If you select all, skip to step 9.

7. Click the drop-down menu to choose where the photos you want to share are stored. Choose the Photos app (on a Mac), the Pictures folder, or another location by selecting Choose folder.

8. In the Albums box, select the photo albums you want to share with your Apple TV.

9. Click Apply (at the bottom right of the screen) to save your changes.

10. On the Apple TV, launch Computers. If you haven't already set up Home Sharing, you'll be asked to sign into your Apple ID.

11. Highlight and select Photos.

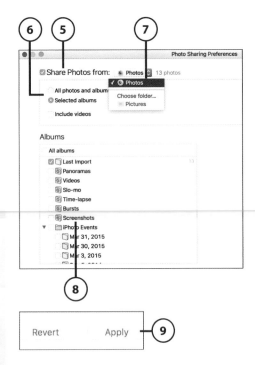

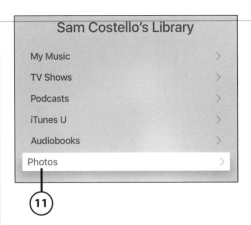

12. On the Photos screen, whatever albums you chose to share in steps 6 and 7 appear. Select the one you're interested in viewing.

13. From the photo album screen, you can use all the features discussed so far: view a single photo by clicking on it, play a slideshow, or use these photos as a screensaver.

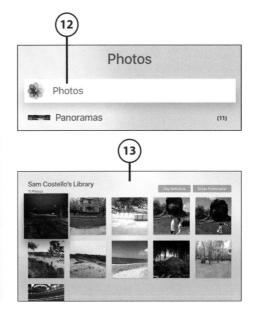

Customizing Your Home Screen Layout

The default arrangement of apps on the Apple TV home screen is the same for everyone, but it doesn't have to stay that way. You can rearrange the apps to fit how you use your Apple TV. For instance, if you never use the iTunes Movies app but use Netflix every day, moving the Netflix app to the top row of your home screen to replace iTunes Movies probably makes sense.

Change the Home Screen Layout

Here's what you need to do to customize the layout of apps on your home screen:

1. Highlight the app you want to move and click and hold the touchpad until the app starts to wiggle.

2. Use the touchpad to move the app to the new location you want to put it in.

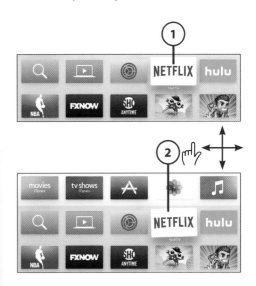

3. When the app is in the new location, click the touchpad to save the new arrangement. The app stops wiggling and stays in its new place on your home screen.

>>>Go Further
HOME SCREEN LAYOUT AFFECTS FEATURED CONTENT

You might have noticed that when you highlight one of the four apps on the first row of your Apple TV home screen, the content displayed at the top of the screen changes. That content is designed to entice you to check out popular offerings within those apps. For instance, highlight the iTunes Movies app and you'll see the most popular movies at iTunes right now.

When you change your home screen layout, the content previewed at the top of the screen changes, too. If you have Netflix on your top row, you'll see recommendations for movies. Put Music there and you'll get selections from your library.

Using Content Restrictions

If you have children in your household, you might have keen interest in this section. The Apple TV comes with a built-in set of features that allows you to control what content can be played on the device and what features are available. This includes movies, TV shows, apps, and more. If you want control over what your kids watch and do on the Apple TV, these are the settings you need to know.

It's Not All Good

Restrictions Apply to Everyone

The Apple TV doesn't have individual user accounts or settings, so it can't distinguish between a 40-year-old and an 8-year-old using it. As a result, when you enable content restrictions, those restrictions apply to everyone using the device. You'll know the password, so you can turn them off when you want something more adult, but it's an extra step.

Enable Content Restrictions

The Apple TV offers a variety of content restriction settings, but before you can configure those, you need to enable content restrictions. Here's how:

1. Launch Settings.

2. Select General.

3. Select Restrictions.

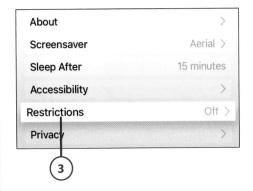

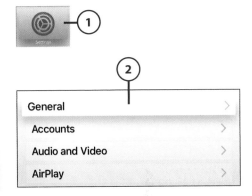

4. In the Parental Controls section, select the Restrictions menu so it toggles to On.

5. Next you set up a four-digit code that locks your restrictions settings and prevents anyone who doesn't know the code from changing them.

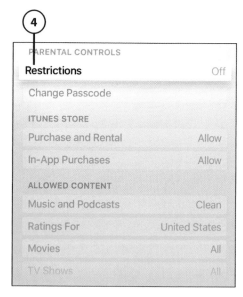

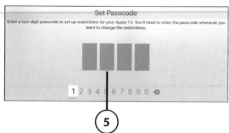

Manage Content Restrictions

After you've turned on content restrictions, here's what they can control:

1. In the iTunes Store section, you can block the rental or purchase of movies and TV shows. Just select the Purchase and Rental menu to toggle it to Restrict.

2. You can also block in-app purchases by selecting that menu to toggle it to Off (see "Managing In-App Purchases and Subscriptions" in Chapter 5, "Using Apps and Games," for more on in-app purchases).

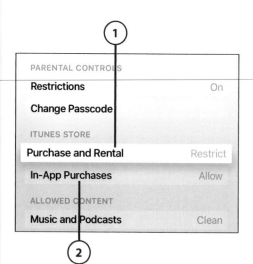

3. The Allowed Content section lets you set limits on the maturity level of the content the Apple TV can play. Select the Music and Podcasts menu and you can allow the following kinds of content: Clean and Explicit. These ratings are based on the information supplied by Apple.

4. In the Ratings For sections, you can use similar ratings for Movies, TV, and Apps.

5. Select the Movies menu and your choice will allow any movie with that rating or a lower one. For instance, select PG-13 and you'll also be able to play PG and G movies.

6. In the TV Shows section, you can choose not to allow TV shows or to allow all TV shows, or to select shows rated anywhere from TV-Y (for basically all audiences) to TV-MA (only for mature audiences).

7. The Apps section uses the ratings assigned to apps by developers. You can restrict all apps, allow all apps, or select apps rated anywhere from 4 years old and up to 17 years old and up.

8. Toggling Siri Explicit Language to Hide will prevent the onscreen Siri menu from displaying explicit language, even if someone speaks in into the microphone.

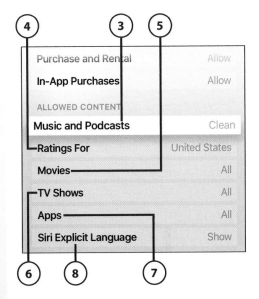

9. In the Game Center section, you can prevent the playing of Multiplayer games by selecting that menu to toggle it to No.

10. You can also block the adding of friends in Game Center the same way.

11. In the Allow Changes section, you can lock the settings for AirPlay and Location Services. Toggle these to Restrict and your current settings will be unchangeable.

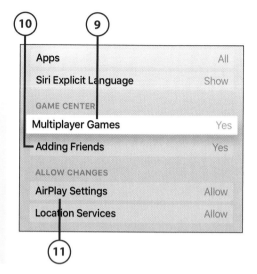

It's Not All Good

The Content Restrictions Can't Block

Content Restrictions' effectiveness is somewhat limited because they can only block content delivered through Apple's platforms (iTunes, Podcasts, App Store, and so on). For example, they can block R-rated movies from iTunes, but not in Netflix. If you've installed non-Apple apps and want to restrict content in them, check those apps to see whether they have similar features. (Netflix, for instance, allows different accounts and settings for kids and adults.)

Turn Off Content Restrictions

After they're enabled, turning off content restrictions is very simple:

1. Launch Settings.

2. Select General.

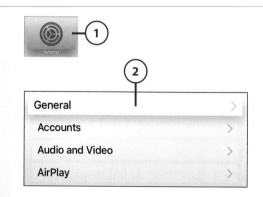

3. Select Restrictions.

4. In the Parental Controls section, select the Restrictions menu to toggle it to Off.

5. Enter your four-digit passcode.

About	>
Screensaver	Aerial >
Sleep After	15 minutes
Accessibility	>
Restrictions	Off >
Privacy	>

PARENTAL CONTROLS

| Restrictions | Off |
| Change Passcode | |

ITUNES STORE

| Purchase and Rental | Allow |
| In-App Purchases | Allow |

Turn off Restrictions

Enter your Apple TV passcode to turn off restrictions.

1 2 3 4 5 6 7 8 9 0

Reset Your Password (and Everything Else)

When you've set up Content Restrictions and protected them with a passcode, the only way to disable the restrictions or change the settings is to know the passcode. But what if you've forgotten your passcode? The only thing you can do, in that case, is reset all the settings on your Apple TV.

To reset your Apple TV settings:

1. Launch Settings.

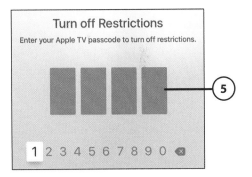

2. Select System.

3. In the Maintenance section, select Reset.

4. Select Reset All Settings.

5. To proceed with the reset, select Reset All Settings.

Last Resort

Resetting your Apple TV settings is a drastic step: It removes all of your accounts, preferences, and customizations. You'll have to set them up again. However, sometimes it's the only option.

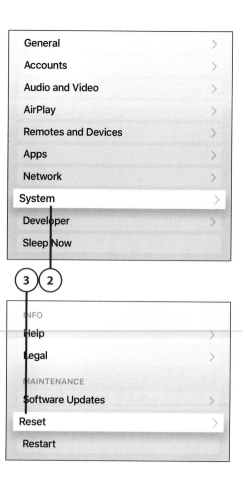

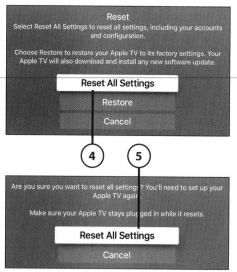

Using AirPlay and AirPlay Mirroring

One of the things Apple is best at is creating a cohesive ecosystem of products that seamlessly work together. If you have an Apple TV and an iPhone, iPad, or Mac, one of the ways you'll benefit from this ecosystem is AirPlay.

AirPlay is an Apple technology that allows you to wirelessly stream audio and video from one device to another compatible device over Wi-Fi. For instance, if you have an AirPlay-compatible speaker that's connected to the same Wi-Fi network as your iPhone, you can send music from your iPhone to that speaker for a better audio experience. It's also a great way for visitors to share their media with you.

Another feature of AirPlay, called Mirroring, allows you to go even further: With it, you can display whatever's on the screen of your iPhone, iPad, or Mac on your HDTV. AirPlay Mirroring turns your TV into an external monitor for your devices, which is great for playing videos and apps you can't get on the Apple TV.

The Apple TV supports AirPlay and AirPlay Mirroring and can receive streaming audio and video from your other Apple products when they're all on the same Wi-Fi network.

Stream Audio from an iPhone or iPad

Sending music or a podcast from your iPhone or iPad to your Apple TV makes a lot of sense. After all, your Apple TV is probably hooked up to a much nicer speaker system than the one available on your mobile device. Follow these steps and you'll be using AirPlay in no time:

1. Make sure your iPhone or iPad is connected to the same Wi-Fi network as your Apple TV.

Both devices must be connected to the same network

2. On your iPhone or iPad, find the music, podcast, or other audio you want to send to the Apple TV.

3. Swipe up from the bottom of the device's screen to reveal Control Center.

4. Tap the AirPlay menu.

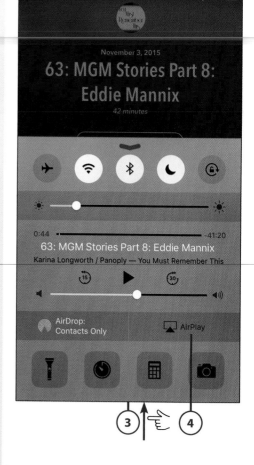

5. In the AirPlay pop-up menu, select your Apple TV.

6. Tap Done. Start playing the audio on your iPhone or iPad and the audio should play through the speakers attached to your Apple TV.

Don't Forget Your Music in the Cloud

AirPlay isn't the only way to get music or other audio that you own to your Apple TV. Remember that any music that you've purchased at iTunes or added to your iCloud account is available in the Apple TV's Music app. Check out "Use Your Full iTunes Library on the Apple TV" in Chapter 6, "Music Television: Music on the Apple TV" for more on how to use this feature.

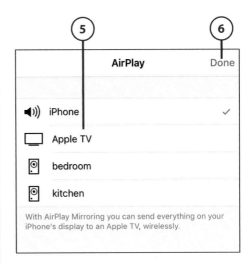

With AirPlay Mirroring you can send everything on your iPhone's display to an Apple TV, wirelessly.

Stream Audio from a Mac

You can stream music or podcasts from your Mac to your Apple TV, too. The technology is the same, but the steps are slightly different:

1. With your Mac and Apple TV on the same network, open iTunes.

2. In iTunes, click the AirPlay icon. (It's the rectangle with the arrow coming into it from the bottom, between the volume slider and the status window at the top.)

3. In the drop-down menu, click Apple TV.

4. When the AirPlay icon is blue to indicate it's enabled, navigate through iTunes to find the music you want to play on your Apple TV.

5. Click the Play/Pause button for your audio on your Mac and it will be sent to the Apple TV.

6. When the music begins playing on your Apple TV, a small window appears in the top-right corner displaying the song, artist, album, and album cover art.

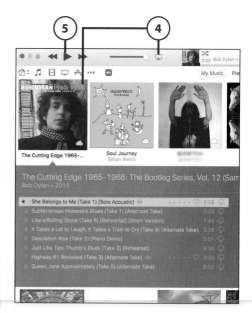

Enable AirPlay Mirroring from an iPhone or iPad

AirPlay is pretty cool by itself, but it gets even cooler and more useful when you add a feature called AirPlay Mirroring, which lets you display whatever's on the screen of your iPhone/iPad or Mac on your HDTV using the Apple TV. To use AirPlay Mirroring:

1. Make sure your iPhone or iPad is connected to the same Wi-Fi network as your Apple TV.

2. On your iPhone or iPad, find the video you want to send to the Apple TV.

3. Swipe up from the bottom of the device's screen to reveal Control Center.

4. Tap the AirPlay menu.

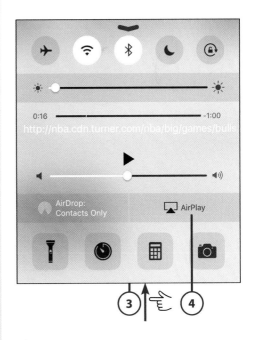

5. In the AirPlay pop-up menu, select your Apple TV.

6. Move the Mirroring slider to On (green).

7. Your iPhone/iPad's screen should now appear on your TV. Use your device however you want to enjoy the content you selected.

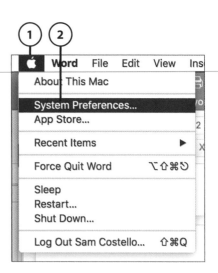

AirPlay Mirroring from a Mac

You can mirror from Macs, too. To do that, ensure both devices are connected to the same network and follow these steps:

1. On your Mac, click the Apple menu.

2. Select System Preferences.

3. Select Displays.

4. Click the AirPlay Display drop-down menu.

5. Select your Apple TV from the drop-down menu. Your Mac's screen should appear on your TV.

Mirroring Shortcut

You can also check the Show mirroring options checkbox on this pop-up window and an AirPlay option appears in the top-right corner of your Mac's menu bar.

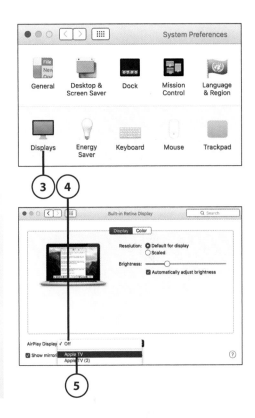

>>>Go Further

AIRPLAY FOR WINDOWS

Although the discussion of AirPlay so far has focused entirely on Macs, Windows users aren't left out of the fun. AirPlay isn't built in to Windows like it is the Mac, so you won't be using the official Apple technology, but with add-on software you can broadcast your PC's screen and audio or video to the Apple TV. Check out these programs to get AirPlay-style functionality:

- **AirParrot**—http://www.airsquirrels.com/airparrot/ **$14.99**

- **5Kplayer**—http://www.5kplayer.com/airplay/airplay-pc-to-apple-tv.htm **Free**

Configure AirPlay Settings

If you use AirPlay often, you should famil-
iarize yourself with the Apple TV settings
that control it. To access them:

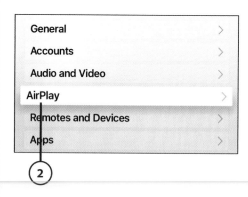

1. Launch Settings.

2. Select AirPlay. The settings on this
   screen function in the following
   ways.

3. **AirPlay**—Toggle this On or Off to
   enable/disable AirPlay entirely.

4. **Apple TV Name**—If you want to
   change the name of your Apple TV
   in AirPlay menus, select this and
   choose one of the preset names or
   add your own custom name.

5. **Play Purchases from iCloud**—If
   you would prefer to play music
   from your iCloud account instead
   of your device or computer, toggle
   this setting to On (if the music isn't
   in your iCloud account it will be
   sent over AirPlay).

6. **AirPlay Display Underscan**—If
   you're mirroring your device and
   the display is cropped, toggle this
   setting to On.

7. **Security**—Turn this setting on to
   prevent unauthorized users from
   using AirPlay to send content to
   the Apple TV (this is useful if you
   use the Apple TV in a public setting). Set a passcode or password
   as your protection.

8. **Require Device Verification**—This
   is another security setting. When
   you toggle it to On, devices that
   want to connect to your Apple TV
   over AirPlay will have to be autho-
   rized using a passcode.

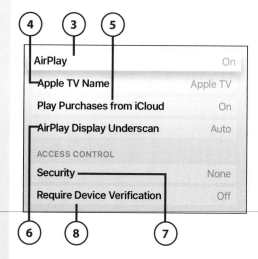

Understanding the Apple TV's Advanced Audio and Video Settings

Most people won't ever need to use the tutorials in this section. These are advanced topics that can help you precisely adjust how your TV and Apple TV work together to display video and play audio. You'll only need to use these if you have particular types of A/V equipment (you'll know if you do) or are an enthusiast for these kinds of topics.

Change HDMI Output Format

It's possible to change the type of video signal being output from your Apple TV to your television via the HDMI port (if you don't know what this means or why you would do it, the chances are very high you don't need to worry about it). To do this:

1. Launch Settings.

2. Select Audio and Video.

3. Select HDMI Output.

4. On the HDMI Output screen, you can choose Auto, YCbCr, RGB High, or RGB Low. Use the touchpad to highlight your choice and click it to make the change.

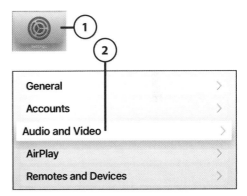

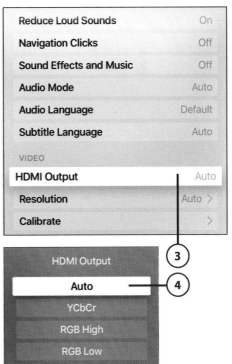

Adjust the Apple TV's Output Resolution

By default, the Apple TV is set to automatically detect the proper video output resolution for the television you're using. However, you might find that changing the resolution improves your picture quality. If so, just follow these steps:

1. Launch Settings.

2. Select Audio and Video.

3. Select Resolution.

4. On the Resolution screen, you can choose from a number of possible screen resolutions. Highlight your choice with the remote and then click the touchpad to change the setting.

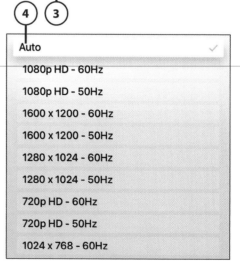

Calibrate Your Television

The default settings of some TVs can cause their pictures to not display properly when using the Apple TV. To calibrate your TV to adjust its picture, do this:

1. Launch Settings.

2. Select Audio and Video.

3. In the Video section, select Calibrate.

4. Use Zoom and Overscan to correct the picture on some TVs extending beyond the edge of the screen. Follow the onscreen instructions to adjust the overscan.

5. Color Bars provides a full-screen image of color bars to allow you to adjust the display of colors to match your preferences.

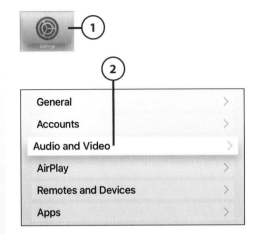

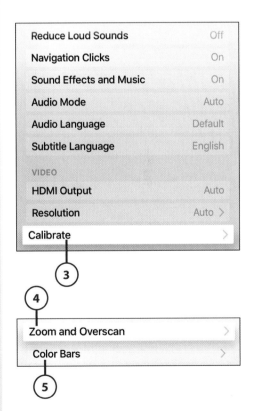

Change Your Audio Mode

The Apple TV, by default, is set to automatically select the best audio mode for your television. Some TVs, though, require 16-bit audio to function properly. To change your Apple TV's audio mode:

1. Launch Settings.

2. Select Audio and Video.

3. Select the Audio Mode menu to toggle it from Auto to 16 bit.

General	>
Accounts	>
Audio and Video	>
AirPlay	>
Remotes and Devices	>
Apps	>

Reduce Loud Sounds	Off
Navigation Clicks	On
Sound Effects and Music	On
Audio Mode	Auto
Audio Language	Default
Subtitle Language	English
VIDEO	
HDMI Output	Auto
Resolution	Auto >
Calibrate	>

Change Your Audio Output

To have the audio sent from your Apple TV to your soundbar, wireless speakers, or Bluetooth headphones instead of your TV or receiver, do this:

1. Launch Settings.

2. Select Audio and Video.

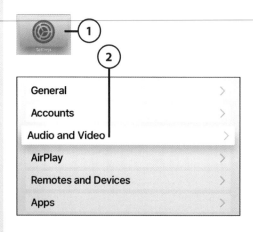

General	>
Accounts	>
Audio and Video	>
AirPlay	>
Remotes and Devices	>
Apps	>

3. In the Audio section, select Audio Output.

4. On the Audio Output screen, highlight and select the device you want to send the audio to. Your Apple TV will start using that device to output audio.

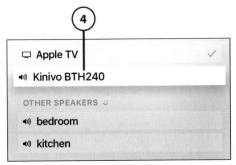

**An example of the beautiful Aerial screensavers Apple created
exclusively for the Apple TV**

The Settings app is full of little options and big changes that can transform how your Apple TV works. Mastering them is the difference between having a standard Apple TV and one customized to your exact needs. In this chapter, you'll learn how to manage your:

→ Screensaver settings

→ Privacy settings

→ Interface settings

→ Accessibility settings

Take Control of Your Apple TV's Settings

With these tips, you'll not only be able to customize how your Apple TV looks and works, but if you have any visual or hearing impairments, you'll be able to access the features of the device to help you get the most out of it.

Setting Your Screensaver

Just like on your computer, the Apple TV has a screensaver built in that turns on when the device has been inactive for a set period of time. This exists both to protect your TV screen—displaying the same image continuously can lead to "burn in," in which the "ghost" of the image appears long after you've started using the TV again—and to provide some visual interest. And this being Apple, there's a lot to be interested in.

You might not choose to stick with them, but all Apple TV users should at least try Apple's built-in video screensavers. That's because they're not typical collages of still pictures moving around the screen. Instead, they're full-screen videos, beautifully produced, that Apple created especially for the Apple TV. Wait until you see them.

The set-up process for the Apple TV covered in Chapter 1, "Introduction to Your Apple TV," included a step where you decided whether to use Apple's included screensavers. Whether you skipped that or prefer using your own images, the next few tutorials can help.

Use Apple's Screensavers

Whether you use Apple's newest video screensavers or their classic stills, you can follow these steps to choose your screensaver (assuming you didn't do that back in Chapter 1):

1. Launch the Settings app.

2. Select General.

3. Select Screensaver.

4. Select Type.

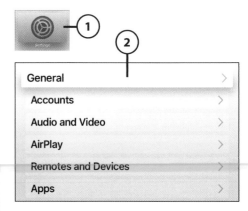

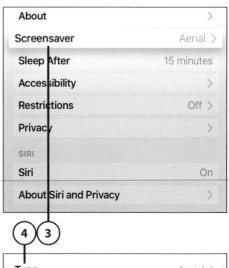

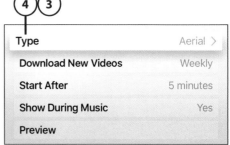

5. On the Type screen, select Aerial to use Apple's full-screen HD video screensavers or Apple Photos to use photography.

6. If you selected Apple Photos, next select the type of photos you prefer (Shot on iPhone 6 is an Apple-curated collection of photos taken by iPhone 6 owners.) Highlight your selection and select it by clicking the touchpad.

7. If you selected Aerial in step 5, you can control how often your Apple TV downloads new screensavers. Select Download New Videos and choose Never, Daily, Weekly, or Monthly.

8. If you selected Apple Photos in step 5, you can control the transition effects used to move from one photo to the next. The full set of options is listed in the Transition section (two options, Ken Burns and Classic, have a second set of options if you select them). Experiment with different transition options to see which you prefer.

9. Return to the Screensaver screen using the Menu button, and highlight Show During Music (this is available no matter which type of screensaver you chose). This controls whether the screensavers are disabled while you listen to music. Selecting the menu toggles it from Yes to No.

Apple automatically updates the video screensavers; there's no need for you to download new ones. And good thing: Each month's new batch is about 500MB. No word yet on whether the photo screensavers will be updated.

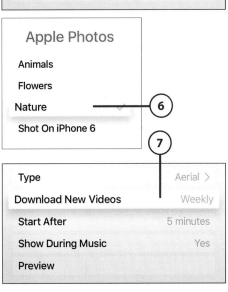

Use Your Photos as Screensavers

You're not required to use Apple's screensavers; you can also use the photos you've taken and stored in your iCloud account. To do that, follow these steps:

1. Launch the Settings app.

2. Select General.

3. Select Screensaver.

4. Select Type.

5. Select either My Photos to use photos accessible through the Photos app on the Apple TV, or Home Sharing to choose photos stored on your computer.

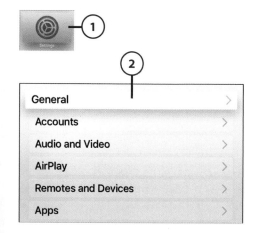

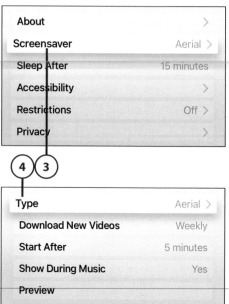

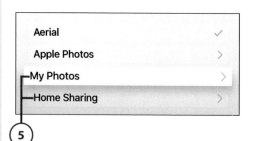

6. Whichever option you select, the next step is to select the photo album that contains the photos you want to use as a screensaver.

7. On the photo album screen, use the touchpad to highlight and select the Set as Screensaver button.

8. A screen asks you to confirm that you want to make the selected photos your screensaver. Highlight and select Yes if you do or No if you've changed your mind.

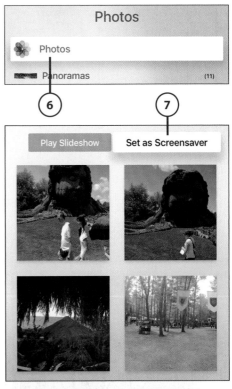

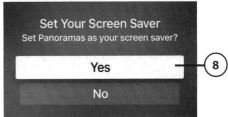

Choose How Quickly Screensavers Appear

By default, the Apple TV's screensaver appears after five minutes of inactivity. You can change that by following these steps:

1. Launch the Settings app.

2. Select General.

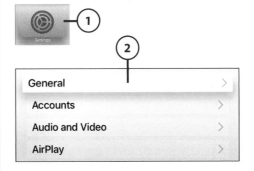

3. Select Screensaver.

4. Select Start After.

5. Set your preference: Never, 2 minutes, 5 minutes, 10 minutes, 15 minutes, or 30 minutes.

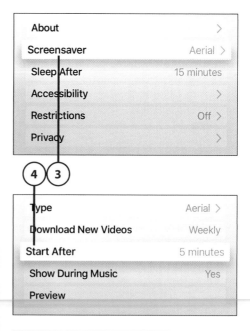

Tweak Your Auto-Sleep Setting

In addition to triggering a screensaver, prolonged periods of inactivity can put the Apple TV to sleep to save power. Control what that period of time is by following these steps:

1. Launch the Settings app.

2. Select General.

3. Select Sleep After.

4. Choose Never, 15 minutes, 30 minutes, 1 hour, 5 hours, or 10 hours.

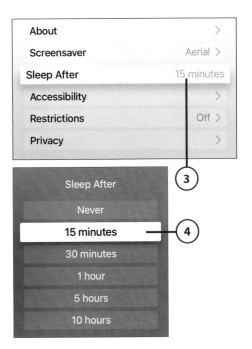

>>>Go Further

START SCREENSAVER IMMEDIATELY

If you don't want to wait for your sleep settings to launch the screensaver, you can start it right away using the Siri Remote. Just click the Menu button twice and your chosen screensaver will display immediately.

Controlling Your Privacy Settings

You don't normally think of needing to protect your privacy when you're watching TV, but with Internet-connected devices like the Apple TV that use apps, you should. There aren't as many privacy settings to concern yourself with as on the iPhone, for instance, but it's worth understanding the options that can help keep your private data private.

Disable Location Services

Location Services is a GPS-style feature that allows the Apple TV to determine where it's located and give you information specific to that area. You'll need this to use features like weather forecasts, to get screensavers that match the time of day, and for some apps and games.

For most people, this is a useful feature that's worth leaving on (which is why it's part of the initial set up process, as discussed in "Set Up Your Apple TV" back in Chapter 1), but if you prefer to disable it, follow these steps:

1. Launch the Settings app.

2. Select General.

3. Select Privacy.

4. Select Location Services.

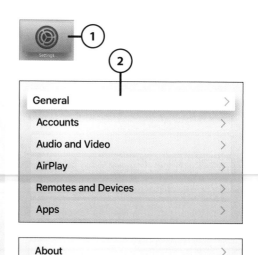

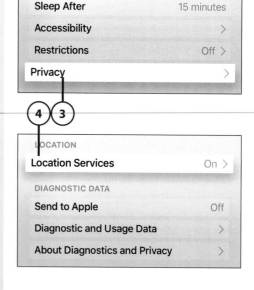

5. On the Location Services screen, select the Location Services menu.

6. Choose Turn Off (or Cancel, if you've changed your mind).

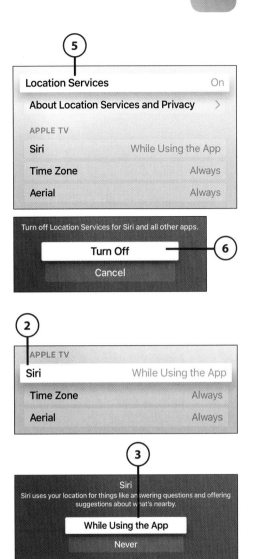

Control Location Services for Individual Apps

You can choose to turn Location Services off entirely, but you can also allow the feature to be used by some apps, and not others. Control which apps can access your location by doing the following:

1. Follow the first four steps in the preceding tutorial.

2. Select one of the apps listed in the Apple TV menu.

3. In the screen that pops up, choose whether to allow Siri to function While Using the App or Never to block it entirely. Repeat these steps for any apps listed on this screen.

Don't Share Diagnostic Data

The Apple TV collects information about how it runs, when apps crash and why, and other low-level technical information. Users can then choose to send that data to Apple to help the company improve future versions of the device. Making a choice about this setting was part of the set-up process back in Chapter 1.

There's no personally identifying information in the data that Apple collects, but you still might prefer to not supply that data to Apple. To turn off the sharing of diagnostic data follow these steps:

1. Launch the Settings app.

2. Select General.

3. Select Privacy.

4. In the Diagnostic Data section, select Send to Apple.

5. Select Don't Send.

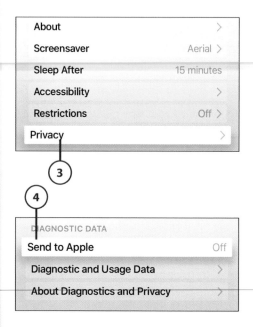

Limit Ad Tracking

Here's a setting that a lot of people don't know about, but will want to change after they do. Advertising networks online and in apps collect tons of data about you to target you with ads. This data includes some personal information, as well as what websites you visit, what apps you use, and more.

If that makes you uncomfortable, and you don't care too much about how specific to you the advertising you see is, you can limit how much ad networks track you. Not all ad networks comply with this setting—users can change the setting, but advertiser compliance is voluntary—but some is better than none.

Limit ad tracking by following these steps:

1. Launch the Settings app.

2. Select General.

3. Select Privacy.

4. In the Advertising section, select Limit Ad Tracking to toggle the menu to On.

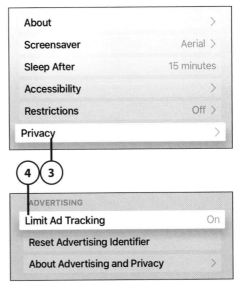

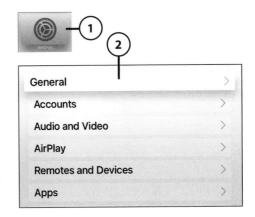

Customizing Interface Settings

The design of the Apple TV's user interface is intended to be modern, sleek, and stylish. For many people, that's true. But for others, the design is full of hard-to-read text, annoying animations, and buttons that are hard to discern from across the living room. If you find yourself more frustrated than pleased by the look of the Apple TV's interface, a few settings can help.

Make Onscreen Text Easier to Read

A common complaint about the text that Apple uses for most of its interfaces these days is that it's too small and too thin, making it hard for some people to see. If you have that complaint, you can improve things by making all text on the Apple TV bold. Just follow these steps:

1. Launch the Settings app.

2. Select General.

3. Select Accessibility.

4. In the Interface section, select Bold Text.

5. On the Restart Required screen, select Continue.

Restart Required

Changing the onscreen text setting requires a restart of your Apple TV. When the device is done rebooting, all onscreen text will be bold—and hopefully easier to read.

Reduce Transparency Effects

Another design flourish that some people complain about reducing legibility is Apple's extensive use of transparency. If you would rather the Apple TV's interface be higher contrast, which makes it easier to distinguish onscreen elements, there's a setting you can change:

1. Launch the Settings app.

2. Select General.

3. Select Accessibility.

4. In the Interface section, select Increase Contrast.

5. Select the Reduce Transparency menu to change it to On.

With that setting changed, you'll see fewer transparency effects and more solid-looking objects onscreen.

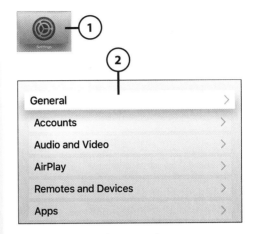

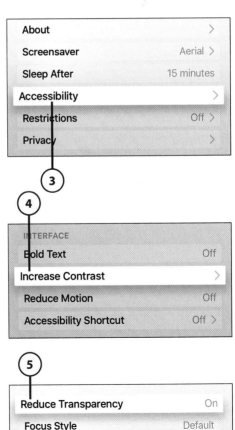

Enable High-Contrast Focus Style

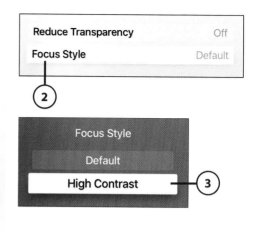

If you reduced transparency in the last section, there's another setting you might prefer: High Contrast Focus Style. When you use the remote to highlight an onscreen item such as a menu, the visual indicator that you've selected the item can be a little subtle: a light background and slight shadow behind the item. To make it easier to see the selector and know what item you're on:

1. Follow the first four steps from the "Reduce Transparency Effects" section.

2. Select Focus Style.

3. Select High Contrast.

Reduce Animations and Motion

For some people, especially those who are very susceptible to motion sickness, all the animations and wiggling and bouncing icons and menus that Apple includes in its interfaces can be unpleasant. Luckily, if you get motion sick—or just don't like all that movement—you can cut down on the animations by following these steps:

1. Launch the Settings app.

2. Select General.

3. Select Accessibility.

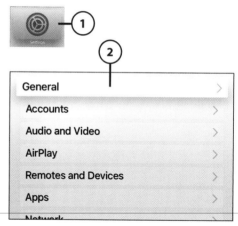

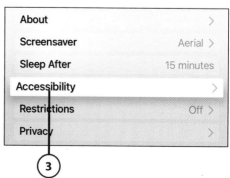

4. In the Interface section, select Reduce Motion so that it toggles to On.

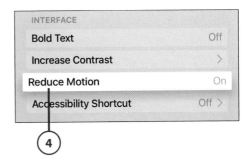

Subtle Changes

The change that this creates is obvious in some cases—movies and TV shows won't shake and twist when you select them in apps anymore—and very subtle in others—app icons switch from small to large, instead of subtly growing and shrinking, when you select them. Overall, though, the Apple TV's interface seems more solid and stable.

Turn Off Navigation Clicks

Each time you move from one item to the next in the Apple TV's menus and apps, a click sound effect plays. The click is there as a subtle bit of feedback to make it clear that you're moving, but you might find it annoying. If you prefer not to hear those clicks, you can disable them this way:

1. Launch the Settings app.

2. Select Audio and Video.

3. In the Audio section, select Navigation Clicks so that the menu toggles to Off.

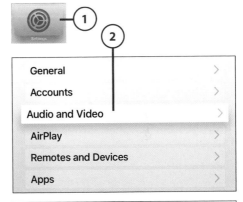

Disable Sound Effects and Music

Do you want to go further in reducing the noises that the Apple TV's interface makes by default? Then you'll want to turn off its built-in sound effects and music, too. Turning them off won't stop you from listening to music or hearing sound effects in games and movies; it just shuts them off when you're navigating menus and apps. To disable them:

1. Launch the Settings app.

2. Select Audio and Video.

3. In the Audio section, select Sound Effects and Music so that the menu toggles to Off.

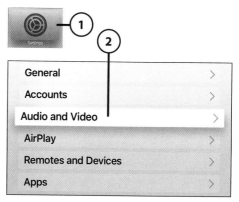

Turn Off Siri

I don't recommend it—without it, you'll lose access to a lot of the Apple TV's coolest features—but you can turn off Siri if you want. To do that, follow these steps:

1. Launch Settings.

2. Select General.

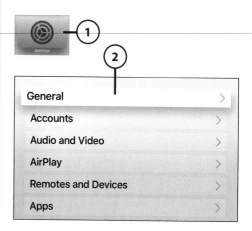

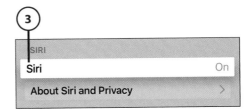

3. Highlight and click the Siri menu with the touchpad to toggle the setting to Off.

Configuring Accessibility Settings

The Apple TV offers a number of features to allow people with visual or hearing impairments to enjoy all the device has to offer. From Closed Captioning to an interface that speaks to you to subtitles and beyond, learn how to enable accessibility features here.

Enable Closed Captions

To turn on Closed Captions for any movie or TV show that offers them, follow these steps:

1. Launch the Settings app.

2. Select General.

3. Select Accessibility.

4. Select Closed Captions and SDH (Subtitles for the Deaf and Hard-of-Hearing) so that it toggles to On.

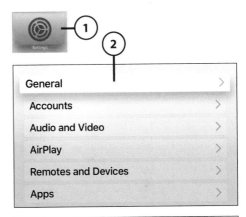

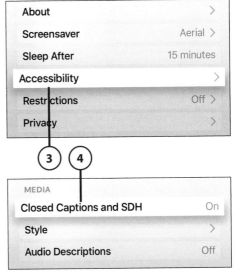

Change the Closed Caption Style

If the default visual appearance of Closed Captions on the Apple TV isn't effective for you, you can make the text bigger, change the font, and even create your own styles. Here's how:

1. Launch the Settings app.

2. Select General.

3. Select Accessibility.

4. Ensure that Closed Captions and SDH is set to On. If it's not, select that menu to toggle it to On.

5. Select Style.

6. The three included styles are Default, Large Text, and Classic. Selecting each one previews the style on the left side of the screen.

7. When you've found the style you want, ensure it's selected (indicated by the check mark) and then you can use the Menu button on the remote to return to the previous screen, the Home button to go back to the main screen, or do anything else. Your selection is saved.

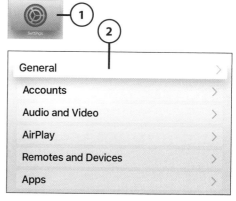

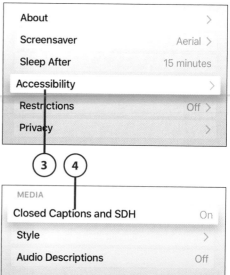

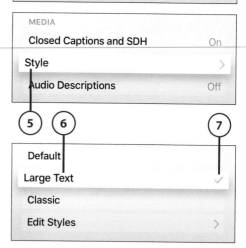

Create a Custom Closed Caption Style

If you don't like the included Closed Caption styles, you can create a version that matches your exact needs and preferences. Here's how:

1. Launch the Settings app.

2. Select General.

3. Select Accessibility.

4. In the Media section, select Style.

5. Select Edit Styles.

6. Select New Style.

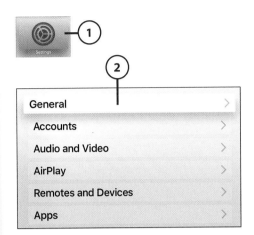

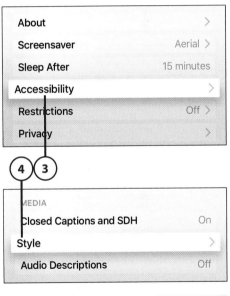

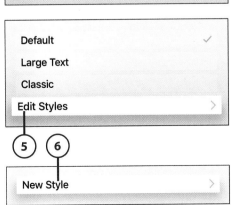

7. Select Description and use the keyboard on the next screen to give the new style a name.

8. In the Text section, choose the font, size, and color of the Closed Caption text.

9. In the Background section, choose the color of the bar behind the text and how transparent that bar will be.

10. In the Advanced section, which is optional, you can choose whether the Closed Caption text will be opaque, whether the text should have effects like drop shadow applied to it, and whether the text will have a color highlight applied to it.

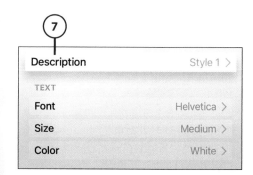

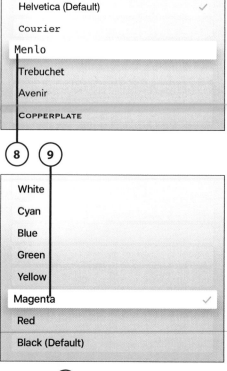

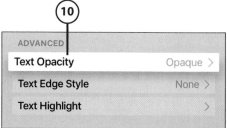

Enable Audio Descriptions

For people with visual impairments, the Audio Descriptions feature allows the Apple TV to read out loud text on the screen and descriptions of content. Although Audio Descriptions aren't available in every app, they're present in the built-in apps and many major third-party apps, making them very useful. Here's how to enable them:

1. Launch the Settings app.

2. Select General.

3. Select Accessibility.

4. In the Media section, select Audio Descriptions so that the menu toggles to On.

Change the Default Subtitle Language

If you regularly use subtitles in a language other than English when watching TV or movies, having to select your preferred language every time might be annoying. You don't have to; just change the default subtitle language and you'll get the language you want every time with fewer clicks. Simply follow these steps:

1. Launch the Settings app.

2. Select Audio and Video.

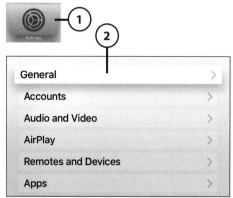

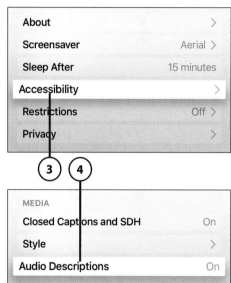

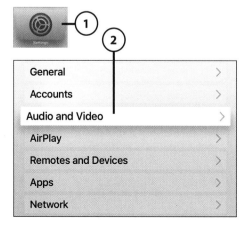

3. Select Subtitle Language.

4. Scroll through the list of languages, highlight the one you want, and select it by clicking the remote's touchpad.

Now, whenever you turn on subtitles—and remember, you can just say "turn on subtitles" to Siri and they'll be there—they will appear in the language you chose.

AUDIO	
Audio Output	Apple TV >
Surround Sound	Auto
Reduce Loud Sounds	Off
Navigation Clicks	On
Sound Effects and Music	On
Audio Mode	Auto
Audio Language	Default
Subtitle Language	English

③

Subtitle Language

Off

Auto

English   — ④

French

German

Japanese

Dutch

Italian

Spanish

Make Apple TV Read Onscreen Text Using VoiceOver

The onscreen menus and text provided by the Apple TV are of very little use to people with some types of visual impairments. If you're in that situation, VoiceOver can help. Similar to the feature with the same name on the Mac and iOS devices, VoiceOver reads onscreen text out loud so that you can know what's there and how to interact with it. Follow these steps to enable VoiceOver:

1. Launch Settings.

 — ①

2. Select General.

3. Select Accessibility.

4. Select VoiceOver from the Vision section.

5. On the VoiceOver screen, select the VoiceOver menu to toggle it to On. After it's on, you can control settings including how fast VoiceOver speaks and its pitch.

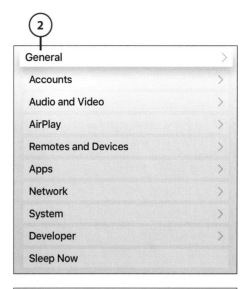

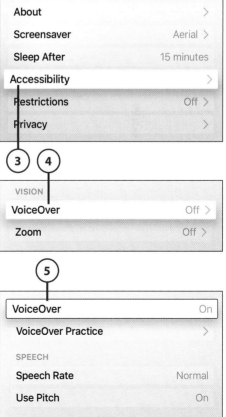

Make Onscreen Elements Bigger with Zoom

Another way accessibility settings can make using the Apple TV easier on the eyes is the zoom feature. When this setting is turned on, the standard user interface of the Apple TV is enlarged—all icons are bigger, all text is bigger, and so on. If you want to squint at the screen less when using your Apple TV, do the following:

1. Launch Settings.

2. Select General.

3. Select Accessibility.

4. Select Zoom from the Vision section.

5. On the Zoom screen, highlight the Zoom menu and toggle it to On by clicking the touchpad.

6. After Zoom is enabled, you can control the maximum zoom level, as well as review the possible zoom gestures located at the bottom-left corner of the screen.

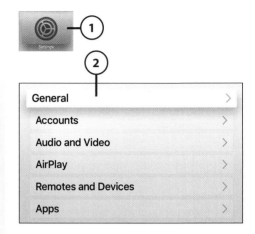

General	>
Accounts	>
Audio and Video	>
AirPlay	>
Remotes and Devices	>
Apps	>

About	>
Screensaver	Aerial >
Sleep After	15 minutes
Accessibility	>
Restrictions	Off >
Privacy	>

VISION

| VoiceOver | Off > |
| Zoom | Off > |

• Press the Touch surface three times to zoom in and out
• Tap and slide with two fingers to adjust zoom level
• Drag to move around the screen
• Tap with two fingers to enable the zoom drag mode
• When zoomed, tap near the edges to move selection

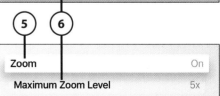

| Zoom | On |
| Maximum Zoom Level | 5x |

Enable Accessibility Shortcut

If you expect to regularly need to change the accessibility settings on your Apple TV, save yourself the clicks and enable this shortcut. When it's turned on, you can turn on your choice of accessibility supports by quickly pressing the Menu button on the remote three times, without ever having to go into the Settings app.

1. Launch the Settings app.

2. Select General.

3. Select Accessibility.

4. In the Interface section, select Accessibility Shortcut.

5. On the Accessibility Shortcut screen, choose what accessibility feature you want to enable by three quick presses of the Menu button: VoiceOver, Zoom, Closed Captions, or Audio Descriptions.

With this preference set, you can turn your selected feature on with three quick presses of the Menu button. It turns off the same way, too.

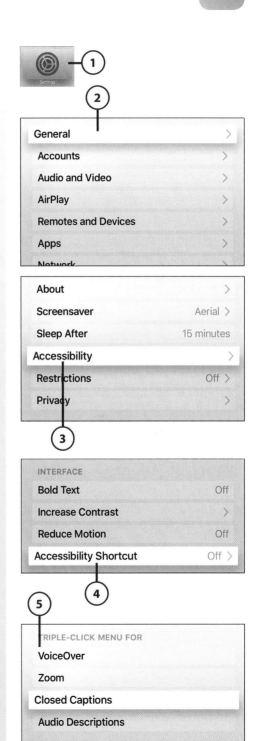

Settings

General >
Accounts >
Audio and Video >
AirPlay >
Remotes and Devices >
Apps >
Network >

About >
Screensaver Aerial >
Sleep After 15 minutes
Accessibility >
Restrictions Off >
Privacy >

INTERFACE
Bold Text Off
Increase Contrast >
Reduce Motion Off
Accessibility Shortcut Off >

TRIPLE-CLICK MENU FOR
VoiceOver
Zoom
Closed Captions
Audio Descriptions

After reading this chapter, you won't get thrown
off track by problems with your Apple TV.

The Apple TV is basically a computer attached to your television, and that means that you might run into computer-type problems when using it. Luckily, in reading this chapter, you'll learn about:

→ Restarting the Apple TV

→ Updating the operating system

→ Resetting or restoring the Apple TV

→ Backing up the Apple TV

→ Fixing problems with your account

→ Solving problems with the Siri Remote

→ Resolving Internet connection issues

→ Getting help from Apple

Troubleshooting Apple TV

After you master these techniques, you'll be able to fix the majority of the day-to-day problems you're likely to run into with your Apple TV.

Restarting the Apple TV

Whenever you encounter a problem on your Apple TV, your first step toward fixing it is the same first step as fixing almost any problem on a computer, smartphone, or tablet: Restart it. Restarting is so effective because it clears out the device's memory (not its permanent storage; just the memory used to run apps), quits apps, and generally resets anything that might be misbehaving. Although not every problem can be solved this way, you'll be surprised at how many are. There are two methods to restart the Apple TV.

Restart the Apple TV Using the Remote

Holding down the right combination of buttons on the Siri Remote can restart the Apple TV from across the room. Just follow these steps:

1. Hold down the Menu and Home buttons on the remote at the same time.

2. Continue to hold them until the light on the front of the Apple TV box begins to blink. At that point, let them go.

3. A second or two later, the Apple TV will begin to restart (not pictured). Wait a little while longer and it brings you back to the home screen after completing the restart.

Restart the Apple TV Using the Settings App

If, for some reason, restarting using the remote doesn't work, you can also restart from the Settings app by following these steps:

1. Launch the Settings app.

2. Select System.

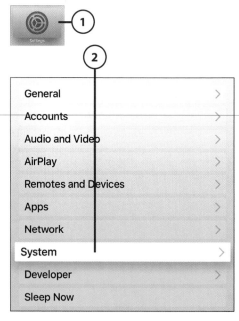

General	>
Accounts	>
Audio and Video	>
AirPlay	>
Remotes and Devices	>
Apps	>
Network	>
System	>
Developer	>
Sleep Now	

3. In the Maintenance section, select Restart.

INFO

Help >

Legal >

MAINTENANCE

Software Updates >

Reset >

Restart

③

>>>*Go Further*

UNPLUGGING IS THE ULTIMATE RESTART

If your Apple TV is so badly locked up that you can't restart it using either of the preceding options, you have another option that always works: Unplug it. Just unplug the Apple TV's power cord, wait 10 or so seconds, and plug it back in again. The Apple TV should boot up as normal. If it doesn't, there's probably a more serious problem with the Apple TV, the power it's receiving, or with its connection to the TV.

Updating the Operating System

The Apple TV runs tvOS, a specialized version of iOS, the operating system that powers the iPhone and iPad. And, just like for those devices, Apple regularly releases updates to tvOS to fix bugs, add new features, update the pre-installed apps, and support new technologies. In short: When there's an update to the Apple TV's operating system, you should install it.

When updates are available, the Apple TV notifies you onscreen. You can also check for updates yourself if an update has been released but you haven't received the notification.

Update tvOS Manually

If you prefer to totally control when you update the Apple TV's operating system, you should perform manual updates. Here's how:

1. Launch the Settings app.

2. Select System.

3. In the Maintenance section, select Software Updates.

4. Select Update Software.

5. The Apple TV checks to see whether a new version of its operating system is available. If there is, you can choose to install it now or to come back and do it later. Select Download and Install and the Apple TV downloads the update, installs it, and restarts itself. How long the process takes depends on the size of the update, the speed of your Internet connection, and the nature of the update. Expect to spend at least 5 minutes (though probably more).

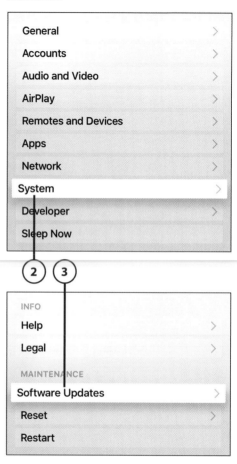

Automatically Update tvOS

Manual updates are just one way to update tvOS. There's no need to follow the earlier steps every time you want to update the OS. Just set it to automatically update itself whenever a new version is released by doing this:

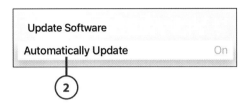

1. Follow the first three steps in the previous task.

2. On the Software Updates screen, select Automatically Update so that the toggle is set to On.

Now, whenever a new update is released, the Apple TV will download and install it without you having to lift a finger.

Resetting or Restoring the Apple TV

In some circumstances you need to remove all the apps you've installed, personal info you've added, and customizations you've made. The two ways you can go about this are:

- **Resetting** the Apple TV's settings can fix problems that have to do with apps, OS preferences, or configuration problems.

- **Restoring** the Apple TV starts you over from scratch; use it to remove your data if you're selling your Apple TV or sending it in for repair. Trying to reset before you restore is always best, because it's such a drastic step.

Reset or Restore the Apple TV

To reset or restore your Apple TV, follow these steps:

1. Launch the Settings app.

2. Select System.

3. In the Maintenance section, select Reset.

4. At this point, you have three options:

   - **Reset All Settings**—This deletes all your accounts, preferences, and customizations, returning the Apple TV to its default status. It doesn't delete apps or downloads.

   - **Restore**—This restores the Apple TV to its factory-new state. It deletes apps, downloads, preferences, and customizations. Essentially, it makes the Apple TV match its status when you first got it.

   - **Cancel**—If you change your mind, the Cancel option lets you back out without selecting anything.

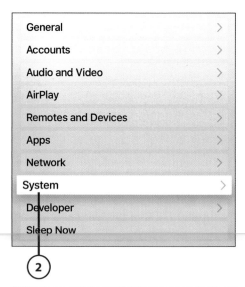

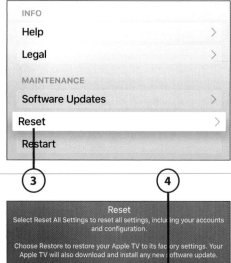

5. If you select Reset All Settings, you need to confirm that you truly want to reset the settings. If you've changed your mind, you can select Cancel. If you proceed, the Apple TV wipes all preferences and you have to set them up again.

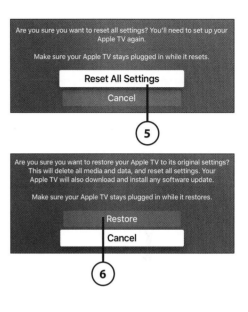

6. If you select Restore, a screen appears that warns you of what happens when you restore to factory settings. If you've changed your mind, select Cancel. If you still want to proceed, select Restore. After the Apple TV restores itself, set it up as if it were brand new, following the steps from "Set Up Your Apple TV" in Chapter 1, "Introduction to Your Apple TV."

Backing Up the Apple TV

Disasters don't happen frequently to our electronics, but when they do, it pays to be prepared. One of the best ways to be prepared for disaster befalling your computer or smartphone is to have a backup. The same is true for your Apple TV. Having a backup of your data, settings, and preferences makes it easier to recover quickly from a problem.

The way backups happen on the Apple TV is very different from what you might be used to from a Mac, iPhone, or iPad. There is no traditional backup with Apple TV, no options to back up data automatically or manually. That's because everything you do is automatically stored in iCloud. All the purchases, downloads, and rentals are listed in your iCloud account and can be accessed whenever you need them.

The only types of data that aren't stored in the cloud are basic preferences like the arrangement of apps on your Apple TV's home screen. As of this writing, there's no way to back up those preferences, but they should be easy enough to re-create if you lose them.

Fixing Problems with Your Account

Because so many things are tied to your Apple ID—your iTunes rentals and purchases, Apple Music, subscriptions to apps like Netflix, and more—problems with your account can mean problems throughout your Apple TV. If you're running into account problems, try the steps in this section to fix them.

Solve Apple ID Problems

A large number of problems with your Apple ID—apps refusing to download or update, subscriptions not being recognized, purchases not playing—can be solved simply by logging out of your Apple ID and back in to it. Follow these steps:

1. Launch Settings.

2. Select Accounts.

3. Select your iCloud account if you can't play music from the cloud or see your Photo Stream content.

4. Select iTunes and App Store if you're having issues with purchases or rentals.

5. Select Game Center if you have problems playing your installed games.

6. Select Home Sharing to resolve problems accessing content accessed through Home Sharing.

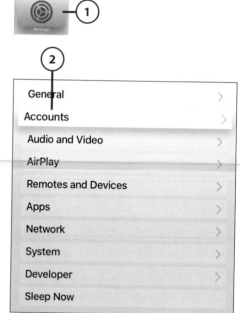

7. Select Sign Out (on the Home Sharing screen, select Turn Off Home Sharing).

8. When you're signed out, sign back in again (or turn on Home Sharing again) and go see whether your problem is solved.

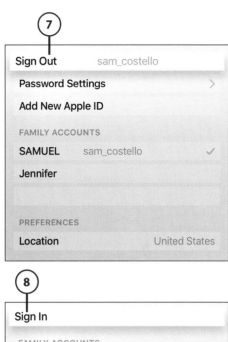

It's Not All Good

Not a Universal Fix

Logging out and back into your Apple ID won't fix every problem every time. Sometimes problems have nothing to do with your Apple ID or, even when they do, they're more complex than logging out and in again can fix. Logging out and back in is a good first step before trying any more-advanced techniques.

Recover a Forgotten Apple ID Password

Another common problem is forgetting your Apple ID password. And it's a real problem, because without it you can't make purchases, download apps, or rent movies. You won't be able to get your current password back, but you can reset the password and choose a new one. Here's how:

1. Using a web browser on your computer or mobile device, go to http://iforgot.apple.com.

2. In the field on that site, enter the email address associated with the Apple ID whose password you want to reset.

3. Click the Next button.

4. Now you must prove that you own the Apple ID whose password you want to reset. This security measure is designed to prevent hackers from stealing control of people's Apple IDs. In this case, you can choose to supply proof either in the form of having Apple email a link to you or answering onscreen the security questions you created when you set up your Apple ID. Make your selection and click Next.

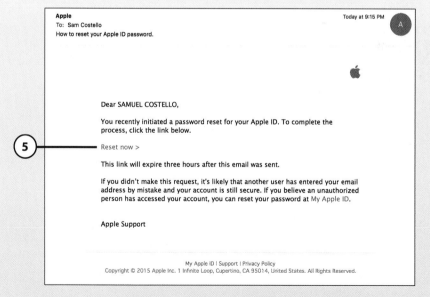

5. If you chose to have Apple email you a link, check your email program and click the Reset Now link in the email Apple sends. Follow the instructions onscreen and then skip to step 7.

6. If you choose to answer questions onscreen, enter your birthday on the first screen and then the answers to your secret questions on the second screen. Click Next to continue.

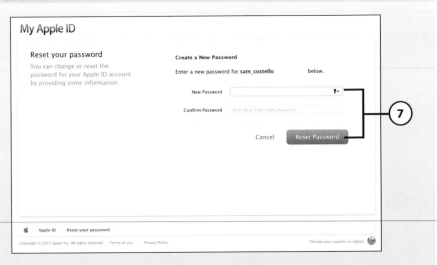

7. On the My Apple ID screen, create a new password for your Apple ID. Enter it twice to make sure you know it and click Reset Password to save the change.

Solving Problems with the Siri Remote

If your Siri remote isn't acting properly, you'll know it right away. After all, there's no mistaking the lack of onscreen response when you click the touchpad or ask Siri a question. If you're facing remote-related troubles, try these fixes.

Charge the Battery

It sounds dumb, but making sure the remote's battery is charged is always a good first step in diagnosing problems with the remote. Low batteries can be the source of all kinds of issues.

Recharge the battery by plugging the cable that came with the Apple TV into the bottom of the remote and into a USB port on a computer or wall adapter (but not on the Apple TV; it can't charge the remote). After an hour or two of recharging, try it; your problem might just be fixed.

What to Do If the Remote Isn't Working

In some instances, the Apple TV's remote might stop working. If you're facing that situation, follow these steps to get it functioning again:

1. Make sure the remote's battery is charged. Check its battery level as described in "How to Tell When Your Battery Is Low," in Chapter 2, "Controlling Your Apple TV: The Remote, Siri, and Search." Recharge it, if needed. If it's got enough power, move on to step 2.

2. Restart the Apple TV. As you learned earlier in this chapter, you can restart the Apple TV with the remote, but if the device isn't responding to the remote, simply unplug the Apple TV from power, wait about 10 seconds and plug it back in again. If that doesn't solve the problem, continue to step 3.

3. Re-pair the remote to the Apple TV. It's possible that your remote has lost its connection to the Apple TV. If so, follow the instructions in "How to Pair the Remote Control with the Apple TV" in Chapter 2.

If the remote still isn't working after all that, you might have a more serious hardware problem. Contact Apple for support. Check out "Getting Help from Apple" later in this chapter for tips on how to do that.

Resolving Internet Connection Issues

Another common source of problems for the Apple TV is its Internet connection. Because the vast majority of things the Apple TV does require the Internet, having a faulty or failed connection is a major problem. Here are a couple of tips for dealing with a flaky network.

Check Your Network Connection

If your Apple TV is acting up in a way that makes you wonder about its Internet connection, you should start by checking its network connection to ensure it's on the right network and has a strong connection. Here's how:

1. Launch Settings.

2. Select Network.

3. In the Connection section, check the Connection menu to make sure your Apple TV is connected to the network you expect via Ethernet or Wi-Fi. If it's not, check out step 5 of "Set Up Your Apple TV" in Chapter 1 for instructions on how to connect to Wi-Fi.

4. In the Status section, check the Signal Strength menu to ensure you have a good connection. Five black dots is the best connection; five empty ones means no connection at all. The fewer black dots you see, the more likely the problem is your connection.

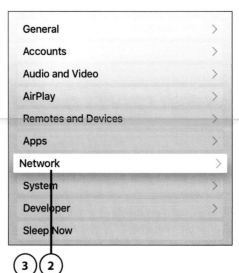

General	>
Accounts	>
Audio and Video	>
AirPlay	>
Remotes and Devices	>
Apps	>
Network	>
System	>
Developer	>
Sleep Now	

CONNECTION

Wi-Fi	Home392 >

STATUS

Network Name	Home392
IP Address	10.0.1.56
Subnet Mask	255.255.255.0
Router	10.0.1.1
DNS	10.0.1.1
Signal Strength	●●●●●
Wi-Fi Address	c8:69:cd:51:83:05

Reset Your Wireless Router

If you've checked your connection strength and found it to be low, your first step to fix it should be to try resetting your wireless router. Your wireless router is the device that takes the Internet connection coming into your home from your cable or phone company and broadcasts it out as Wi-Fi. Without it, there would be no Wi-Fi network in your home to connect to.

The easiest way to reset your router is to follow these steps:

1. Unplug it from the power.

2. Wait 10 seconds.

3. Plug it back in.

4. Let the router boot up and the Apple TV connect to it.

5. Check your connection strength using the steps outlined above. If you've got more black dots, you should be good to go. If not, move on to the next step.

Combination Modem/Routers

Depending on your Internet service provider and choices you made during sign up and installation, it's possible that you have a single device that combines the cable modem and router, rather than two separate devices. If that's your situation, resetting that device is the same as resetting either of the standalone boxes.

Reset Your Cable Modem

Your cable modem is the device that connects to the Internet jack in the wall and is provided to you by your cable or phone company when you sign up for Internet service. It's the thing that brings the Internet into your house. You can connect a wireless router to it or directly attach the Apple TV.

If you're not getting a good—or any—Internet connection, reset it by following these steps:

1. Unplug the cable modem from the power.

2. Wait 10 seconds.

3. Plug it back in again.

It generally takes a minute or two for the cable modem to connect to the Internet again and then, if you have a router that connects to your modem, for it to begin passing data back and forth to it.

When everything is restarted, though, you should have a fresh, working Internet connection.

Internet Service Outages

If you're having trouble with your Apple TV's Internet connection and none of these steps have solved it, make sure there's not an Internet outage in your area. Try getting online with another device on your home network. If that device doesn't work either, call your Internet service provider to see if they can help.

Getting Help from Apple

If you've tried the tips in this chapter and your problem still isn't solved, and there's nothing wrong with your Internet connection, your best bet is to contact the experts—Apple. You can do this at their stores or on the phone.

The Apple TV's Warranty

The warranty and support period that comes with every Apple TV is one year of hardware coverage and 90 days of phone support. You can extend that by an additional 1 year of hardware coverage and to 2 full years of phone support by purchasing an AppleCare extended warranty for US$29 as of this writing. If you don't have AppleCare and need help outside of those initial periods, expect to pay Apple for the help.

Get Help at the Apple Store

One place to get help from Apple is the same place you might have bought your Apple TV: your local Apple Store. The Genius Bar at each Apple Store is stocked with people trained to diagnose and resolve problems with Apple products, so that's where you need to go.

With the popularity of Apple products, there's often a long wait to see a Genius. Make an appointment and you won't have to wait. Here's how:

1.   In a web browser on your computer or mobile device, go to http://support.apple.com.

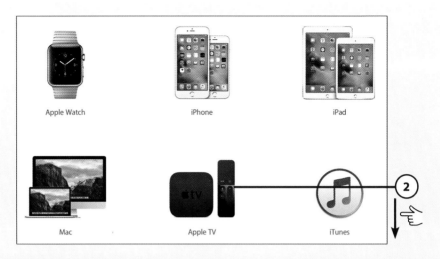

Apple Watch   iPhone   iPad

Mac   Apple TV   iTunes

2.   Scroll down and select Apple TV.

3.   The Welcome screen offers you access to all of Apple's instructional and troubleshooting content for the Apple TV. There's lots of useful information to check out here, but for now, select Contact Support.

4. Select the type of trouble you're having with your Apple TV. It's important to know here that the type of trouble you're having determines the type of support you get. Software and configuration problems are generally handled by Apple over the phone. If you're having hardware problems, making an in-store appointment is an option.

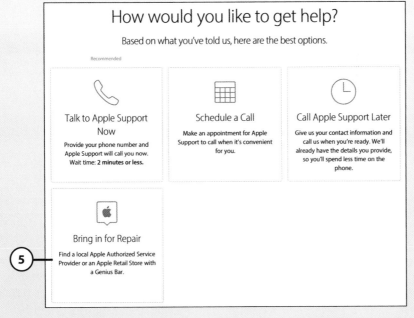

5. Choose what type of support you prefer. You can have Apple call you, schedule a call, or call Apple when you have time. For the purposes of this tutorial, though, select Bring in for Repair.

6. To determine where to bring your Apple TV for repair, you need to share your location with Apple. If Apple can determine your location, the field in the center of the screen reads "Current Location." If it's empty, enter your city and state or ZIP Code. Click Go.

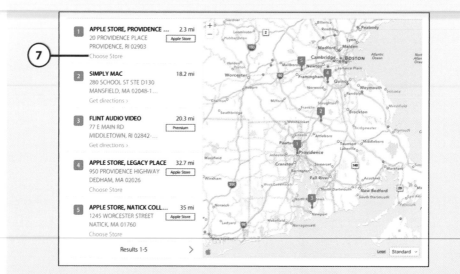

7. Based on your location, Apple provides a list of nearby Apple Stores and approved repair facilities. Find the one you want to go to and click the Choose Store link beneath it.

8. To book an appointment, you need to have an Apple ID. Sign in with yours here.

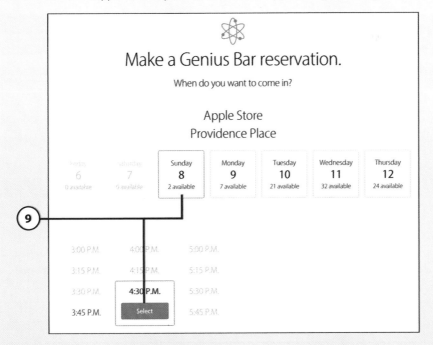

9. Select the date and time for your appointment. Begin by picking a day. Each day shows how many available appointments there are. Click on a day to choose it. Pick a time from the list. Click the Select button to pick your time slot.

Contact Apple Support

Hello, SAMUEL COSTELLO   Sign out

Your reservation is confirmed.

What: Genius Bar reservation
Why: Apple TV, Remote & Accessories
When: Sunday, November 8, 2015 at 4:30 p.m.
Where: APPLE STORE, PROVIDENCE PLACE
Case ID: 981892393

⊕ Add a Comment

Reschedule   Cancel

10. The next screen confirms your appointment. An email confirmation should arrive a few minutes later.

Get Phone Support from Apple

If you don't have an Apple Store nearby, or prefer not to have to leave the house to get help with your issue, you can call Apple. The same warranty terms as noted previously apply here.

To get support by phone in the United States, call Apple at 1-800-275-2273, or follow the steps from the last tutorial in this chapter to schedule a call at a specific time.

Index

Symbols

3D effects on remote control, 40
5Kplayer, 231
7 Minute Workout app, 167

A

A8 processor, 16
accelerometer (remote control), 19
accessibility settings. *See also* interface settings
  accessibility shortcut, enabling, 263
  Audio Descriptions, enabling, 259
  closed captions
    changing default language, 259-260
    changing style of, 256
    creating custom style, 257-258
    enabling, 255
  onscreen text
    adjusting zoom levels, 262
    reading with VoiceOver, 260-261

accessibility shortcut, enabling, 263
accessing
  music
    via Home Sharing, 172
    via iTunes, 170-171
  recent apps, 41
accounts
  Apple ID, creating, 9
  HBO GO, signing in, 108-110
  HBO NOW, signing in, 110
  Hulu, signing in, 126-127
  iCloud, 9, 12
  iCloud Photos, signing in, 212-213
  Netflix, signing in, 98
  network TV apps, signing in, 94-97
  Showtime, signing in, 119-120
  Showtime Anytime, signing in, 117-118
activating. *See* enabling
ad tracking, limiting, 249
adding
  Apple Music songs to iTunes Music Library, 180-181

movies/TV shows
  to HBO Watchlist, 114
  to My List in Showtime apps, 123-124
  to Netflix queue, 102
adjusting. *See* changing
Air Wings game, 166
AirParrot, 231
AirPlay, 225
  configuring, 232
  streaming audio
    from iPhone/iPad, 225-227
    from Mac, 227-228
  for Windows, 231
AirPlay Mirroring, 225
  enabling
    from iPhone/iPad, 229-230
    from Mac, 230-231
Amazon Prime Video, 97
animation, reducing onscreen, 252-253
App Detail Screen (App Store), 140-141
AppleCare extended warranty, 280
Apple ID, 8-9
  creating, 9
  downloading apps, 142
  resetting password, 274-276
  signing in/out, 272-273
Apple Music, 177. *See also* streaming, music
  canceling, 178-179
  new releases, 196-197
  radio stations
    Beats 1, 197-199
    curated stations, 199-201
    custom stations, 201-203
    modifying song selections, 203-204
  recommendations from, 195
    improving, 196

songs
  adding to iTunes Music Library, 180-181
  deleting from iTunes Music Library, 182-183
  marking as favorite, 188-189
  subscribing, 178
Apple remote. *See* remote control
Apple resources for help, 280
  Apple Store, 281, 286
  phone support, 286
Apple screensavers, selecting, 240-241
Apple Store, help from, 281, 286
Apple TV
  backing up, 271
  Bluetooth game controllers, pairing, 45-46
  Bluetooth headphones, pairing, 44
  cable TV and, 6-8, 94
  described, 5-6
  home screen apps, 24-25
  keyboard support, 45
  optional items
    Ethernet cable, 11
    game controllers, 14
    home theater system, 11-12
    iCloud account, 12
    iPhone/iPad/iPod touch, 12
    Remote Loop, 13-14
    surge protector, 10-11
  remote control. *See* remote control
  requirements, 7
    Apple ID, 8-9
    broadband Internet connection, 7
    HDMI cable, 8
    high-definition TV, 7
  resetting/restoring, 269-271
  restarting, 265
    with remote control, 266
    with Setting app, 266
    by unplugging, 267

setup
    Ethernet versus Wi-Fi, 16
    home theater connections, 17
    with iPhone/iPad, 23-24
    pairing remote control, 33
    ports and connectors, 15-16
    with remote control, 20-22
    third-party remote controls, 34-35
sleep mode
    activating with remote control, 29
    waking from, 29
updating operating system, 267
    automatically, 269
    manually, 268
warranty, 280
app slicing, 148
App Store, 25
    App Detail Screen, 140-141
    browsing, 138-139
    buying apps, 142-143
    renting apps, 143
    requesting refunds, 147
    reviewing apps, 150-151
    saving password, 143-145
    searching, 138
apps. *See also* games
    7 Minute Workout, 167
    App Detail Screen, 140-141
    browsing App Store, 138-139
    buying, 142-143
    deleting, 145-146, 149
    downloading
        Apple ID, 142
        saving password, 143-145
    enabling Location Services for, 247
    on home screen, 24-25
        customizing layout, 217-218
    in-app purchases, 160
        buying, 160-161
        disabling, 161-162
        enabling, 162

iTunes Movies. *See* movies
launching with Siri, 53
Madefire, 165
for music, 206-208
Photos
    selecting screensavers, 242-243
    viewing photos/videos, 213-217
    viewing slideshows, 214-215
Podcasts by MyTuner, 167
recent apps, accessing, 41
redownloading, 146
refunds on, 147
Remote app, 46
    limitations, 49
    setup, 47-48
    usage, 48-49
renting, 143
reviewing at App Store, 150-151
Search, 60
searching App Store, 138
searching within, 64
Settings. *See* settings
storage management, 148-149
streaming, 148
subscriptions, 159
    managing, 162-163
universal search support, 57
updating, 163-164
video apps. *See* movies; Netflix; network
    TV apps; TV shows
asking questions with Siri, 53
audio
    Audio Descriptions, enabling, 259
    navigation clicks, disabling, 253
    sound effects/music (in navigation),
        disabling, 254
    streaming
        from iPhone/iPad, 225-227
        from Mac, 227-228

audio books, playing, 205

Audio Descriptions, enabling, 259

audio mode, changing, 236

audio output settings, changing, 236-237

automatic app updates, enabling, 164

automatically updating tvOS operating
  system, 269

automatically uploading photos to iCloud,
  212

B

backing up Apple TV, 271

battery in remote control
  charging, 42, 277
  length of charge, 40
  low charge level, 42-43
  replacing, 42

Beats 1 radio station, 197
  listening to, 198
  requesting songs, 199
  show schedule, 197

Bluetooth, 16, 23
  game controllers, pairing, 45-46
  headphones, pairing, 44
  keyboards, Apple TV support, 45
  remote control, 32

bold text, changing onscreen text to, 250

broadband Internet connections, 7

browsing
  App Store, 138-139
  iTunes Music Library, 173-174
  movies via iTunes, 69-70
  TV shows via iTunes, 80-81

built-in apps, deleting, 149

buying
  apps, 142-143
  in-app purchases, 160-161

movies via iTunes, 71-73

TV shows
  via iTunes, 82
  Season Pass, 83

C

cable modem, resetting, 279-280

cable TV, Apple TV and, 6-8, 94

cables. *See also* connections
  Ethernet, 11
  HDMI, 7-8
  ports for, 15-16

calibration settings, 235

canceling
  Apple Music, 178-179
  subscriptions, 162-163

CBS All Access, cost of, 97

challenging friends to games, 156-157

changing
  audio mode, 236
  audio output settings, 236-237
  closed caption style, 256
  default closed caption language,
    259-260
  HDMI output format, 233
  onscreen text to bold, 250
  output resolution, 234
  screensaver timing, 243-244
  sleep mode timing, 244-245
  song selections on radio stations,
    203-204
  third-party remote control settings, 36
  volume (Reduce Loud Sounds feature),
    75

charging remote control battery, 42, 277

children, content restrictions. *See* content
  restrictions

clicks (in navigation), disabling, 253

closed captions
    changing default language, 259-260
    changing style of, 256
    creating custom style, 257-258
    enabling, 51, 78, 255
commands (Siri), frequently used, 51-55
Computers app, 25
configuring. *See also* customizing; setup
    AirPlay, 232
    Remote app, 47-48
connections. *See also* cables; pairing
    Internet
        broadband, 7
        dial-up, 7
        resetting cable modem, 279-280
        resetting wireless router, 279
        troubleshooting, 278
    to home theater systems, 17
content restrictions, 218
    disabling, 222-223
    enabling, 219-220
    limitations on, 222
    managing, 220-222
    resetting passcode, 223-224
cost
    Hulu, 126
    network TV apps with streaming
        services, 97
creating Apple ID, 9
cross-device game playing, 152
curated radio stations, 199-201
    modifying song selections, 203-204
custom closed caption style, creating,
    257-258
custom radio stations
    creating, 201-203
    deleting, 204
    modifying song selections, 203-204
customizing. *See also* configuring
    home screen, 217-218

screensavers, 239
    Apple screensavers, 240-241
    from Photos app, 242-243
    timing for, 243-244
    sleep mode, timing for, 244-245

D

Daily Burn app, 132
data limits on Internet service plans, 6
default closed caption language, changing,
    259-260
deleting. *See* removing
diagnostic data sharing, disabling, 247-248
dial-up Internet connections, 7
disabling
    content restrictions, 222-223
    diagnostic data sharing, 247-248
    game invitations, 155
    in-app purchases, 161-162
    Location Services, 245-247
    movie subtitles, 78
    navigation clicks, 253
    Siri, 254
    sound effects/music (in navigation), 254
downloading apps
    Apple ID, 142
    multiple times, 146
    saving password, 143-145

E

editing. *See* changing
enabling
    accessibility shortcut, 263
    AirPlay Mirroring
        from iPhone/iPad, 229-230
        from Mac, 230-231

Audio Descriptions, 259

automatic app updates, 164

closed captions, 51, 78, 255

content restrictions, 219-220

high-contrast selectors, 252

Home Sharing, 89-90

in-app purchases, 162

Location Services by app, 247

Photo Stream, 212

remote control for TV/home theater system control, 26

Siri, 50

sleep mode with remote control, 29

VoiceOver, 260-261

equalizing music volume, 193-194

Ethernet

cables, 11

port, 15

Wi-Fi versus, 16

F

Family Sharing, 87

fast forward

with remote control, 39

with Siri, 52

favorite songs, marking in Apple Music, 188-189

featured content on home screen, 218

featured releases, browsing, 69

finding. *See* browsing; searching

fixing problems. *See* troubleshooting

For You section (Apple Music), recommendations from, 195

improving, 196

forgotten password, resetting, 274-276

free apps, password settings, 145

free Hulu app, 126

frequently used Siri commands, 51-55

friends, challenging to games, 156-157

Funny Or Die app, 133

G

Galaxy on Fire: Manticore Rising game, 166

Game Center

challenging friends to games, 156-157

checking high scores, 155

multiplayer games, 157-159

signing in, 154-155

game controllers, 14

Bluetooth controllers, pairing with Apple TV, 45-46

iPhone as, 12

Remote app and, 49

remote control as, 40

games. *See also* apps

Air Wings, 166

Galaxy on Fire: Manticore Rising, 166

Guitar Hero Live, 165

in-app purchases, 160

buying, 160-161

disabling, 161-162

enabling, 162

playing, 151

challenging friends, 156-157

checking high scores in Game Center, 155

cross-device playing, 152

disabling game invitations, 155

multiplayer games, 157-159

with remote control, 152-153

sending game invitations, 157

signing into Game Center, 154-155

with third-party controllers, 153

streaming, 148

genre of movies, browsing by, 69-70

Guitar Hero Live game, 165

gyroscope (remote control), 19

H

HBO GO app, 107
  adding items to Watchlist, 114
  searching, 113
  signing in, 108-110
  watching, 115-117
HBO NOW app, 107
  adding items to Watchlist, 114
  cost, 97
  searching, 113
  signing in, 110
  subscribing to, 111-112
  watching, 115-117
HDMI cables, 7-8
HDMI-CEC support, 27
HDMI output format, changing, 233
HDMI port, 15
headphones (Bluetooth), pairing with Apple TV, 44
help resources, 280
  Apple Store, 281, 286
  phone support, 286
high-contrast selectors, enabling, 252
high-definition TVs, 7
high scores, checking in Game Center, 155
Home button (remote control), 18
  recent apps, accessing, 41
home screen
  apps, 24-25
  customizing, 217-218
  featured content, 218
Home Sharing, 88
  accessing music via, 172
  enabling, 89-90
  viewing photos/videos, 215-217
  watching movies/TV shows, 90-91

home theater systems, 11-12
  connecting to, 17
  controlling with remote control, 26
Hulu app, 126
  searching, 129-130
  signing in, 126-127
  subscribing, 127-128
  watching shows, 130-131

I-J

iCloud
  accessing iTunes Music Library, 170-171
  accounts, 9, 12
iCloud Photos, 211
  enabling Photo Stream, 212
  signing in, 212-213
improving Apple Music recommendations, 196
in-app purchases, 160
  buying, 160-161
  disabling, 161-162
  enabling, 162
information about movies, viewing, 76
interface settings
  changing to bold text, 250
  disabling
    navigation clicks, 253
    Siri, 254
    sound effects/music, 254
  enabling high-contrast selectors, 252
  reducing
    animation/motion, 252-253
    transparency, 251
Internet connections, troubleshooting, 278
  resetting cable modem, 279-280
  resetting wireless router, 279
Internet service plans
  data limits, 6
  speed of connection, 7

invitations (games)
  disabling, 155
  sending, 157
iOS devices, 12
  Apple TV setup, 23-24
  continuing gameplay on, 152
  enabling AirPlay Mirroring, 229-230
  Remote app, 46
    limitations, 49
    setup, 47-48
    usage, 48-49
  streaming audio from, 225-227
IR (infrared) port, 16, 19
iTunes
  Home Sharing, enabling, 90
  movies, 24
    browsing, 69-70
    enabling subtitles, 78
    Movie Detail screen, 71
    pre-ordering, 73
    Reduce Loud Sounds feature, 75
    renting/buying, 71-73
    searching for, 68
    viewing information about, 76
    watching, 74-77
  Music Library
    accessing via Home Sharing, 172
    accessing via iCloud, 170-171
    adding Apple Music songs to, 180-181
    browsing, 173-174
    deleting Apple Music songs from, 182-183
    searching, 175
  TV shows, 24
    browsing, 80-81
    buying, 82
    buying Season Pass, 83
    enabling subtitles, 78
    getting Season Pass episodes, 84
    searching for, 79-80
    watching, 84, 87
  iTunes Match, 171

K

keyboards, Apple TV support, 45
kids, content restrictions. *See* content
  restrictions

L

language of closed captions, changing
  default, 259-260
launching apps with Siri, 53
Lifetime Movie Club, cost of, 97
Lightning port (remote control), 19
limits on Internet service plans, 6
listening to music. *See* playing, music
Location Services
  disabling, 245-247
  enabling by app, 247
logging in/out. *See* signing in
low charge level (remote control), 42-43

M

Mac
  enabling AirPlay Mirroring, 230-231
  streaming audio from, 227-228
Madefire app, 165
managing
  content restrictions, 220-222
  storage, 148-149
  subscriptions, 162-163
manually updating tvOS operating system, 268
marking favorite songs in Apple Music, 188-189

memory, 16. *See also* storage management

Menu button (remote control), 18

microphone (remote control), 17

Mirroring. *See* AirPlay Mirroring

MLB.com At Bat app, 133

modem, resetting, 279-280

modifying. *See* changing

motion, reducing onscreen, 252-253

Motion Comics, 165

Movie Detail screen, 71

movie quotes, saying to Siri, 53

movies. *See also* video apps

    adding

        to HBO Watchlist, 114

        to My List in Showtime apps, 123-124

        to Netflix queue, 102

    browsing via iTunes, 69-70

    enabling subtitles, 78

    information about

        obtaining with Siri, 52

        viewing, 76

    Movie Detail screen, 71

    organizing in Netflix queue, 103

    pre-ordering via iTunes, 73

    rating content in Netflix, 106

    Reduce Loud Sounds feature, 75

    removing from Netflix queue, 103

    renting/buying via iTunes, 71-73

    searching for

        via HBO apps, 113

        via Hulu, 129-130

        via iTunes, 68

        via Netflix, 101-102

        via Showtime apps, 122-123

    watching

        via HBO apps, 115-117

        via Home Sharing, 90-91

        via Hulu, 130-131

        via iTunes, 74-77

        via Netflix, 104-106

        via Showtime apps, 124-125

moving apps on home screen, 217-218

multiplayer games, 157-159

music

    apps, 206-208

    marking as favorite in Apple Music, 188-189

    new releases from Apple Music, 196-197

    owned music, 169

        accessing via Home Sharing, 172

        accessing via iTunes, 170-171

        browsing, 173-174

        in iTunes Match, 171

        searching, 175

    playing, 184

        Beats 1 radio station, 198

        curated radio stations, 199-201

        custom radio stations, 201-203

        playback screen options, 185-187

        playlists, 192-193

        shuffling, 189-192

        Sound Check feature, 193-194

    recommendations from Apple Music, 195-196

    streaming, 169. *See also* Apple Music

        adding songs to iTunes Music Library, 180-181

        canceling Apple Music, 178-179

        deleting songs from iTunes Music Library, 182-183

        subscribing to Apple Music, 178

Music app, 25. *See also* music

music (in navigation), disabling, 254

My List (Showtime), adding items to, 123-124

N

navigation clicks, disabling, 253

NBA League Pass app, 134

Netflix, 98

    adding shows to queue, 102

    organizing queue, 103

    rating content, 106

    removing shows from queue, 103

    searching, 101-102

    signing in, 98

    subscribing to, 99-101

    watching movies/TV shows, 104-106

network connections. *See* Internet connections

network TV apps, 8, 93-94

    cable TV and, 94

    signing in, 94-97

    streaming services, 97

new releases from Apple Music, 196-197

New section (Apple Music), 196-197

Nickelodeon Noggin, cost of, 97

O

onscreen text

    changing to bold, 250

    enabling high-contrast selectors, 252

    reading with VoiceOver, 260-261

    reducing

        animation/motion, 252-253

        transparency, 251

    zoom levels, 262

operating systems. *See* tvOS operating system

optional items for Apple TV

    Ethernet cable, 11

    game controllers, 14

    home theater system, 11-12

    iCloud account, 12

    iPhone/iPad/iPod touch, 12

    Remote Loop, 13-14

    surge protector, 10-11

organizing Netflix queue, 103

output format (HDMI), changing, 233

output resolution, changing, 234

output settings for audio, changing, 236-237

owned music, 169

    accessing

        via Home Sharing, 172

        via iTunes, 170-171

    browsing, 173-174

    in iTunes Match, 171

    searching, 175

P

paid apps

    redownloading, 146

    refunds on, 147

pairing

    Bluetooth game controllers, 45-46

    Bluetooth headphones, 44

    remote control, 33

    third-party remote controls, 34-35

parental control. *See* content restrictions

passcodes, resetting, 223-224

passwords

    Apple ID, resetting, 274-276

    saving in App Store, 143-145

phone support, help from, 286

Photo Stream, enabling, 212

photos

    iCloud Photos, 211

        enabling Photo Stream, 212

        signing in, 212-213

    uploading to iCloud, 212

viewing, 213
   with Home Sharing, 215-217
   as slideshow, 214-215
Photos app, 25
  screensavers, selecting, 242-243
  viewing photos/videos, 213
   with Home Sharing, 215-217
   as slideshow, 214-215
playback screen options (music), 185-187
playing
  audio books, 205
  games, 151
   challenging friends, 156-157
   checking high scores in Game Center, 155
   cross-device playing, 152
   disabling game invitations, 155
   multiplayer games, 157-159
   with remote control, 152-153
   sending game invitations, 157
   signing into Game Center, 154-155
   with third-party controllers, 153
  music, 184
   Beats 1 radio station, 198
   curated radio stations, 199-201
   custom radio stations, 201-203
   playback screen options, 185-187
   playlists, 192-193
   shuffling, 189-192
   Sound Check feature, 193-194
  podcasts, 205
playlists (music)
  creating, 193
  playing, 192-193
Play/Pause button (remote control), 18
podcasts, playing, 205
Podcasts by MyTuner app, 167
ports, 15-16
power supply, 15

pre-ordering movies via iTunes, 73
privacy settings
  ad tracking, limiting, 249
  diagnostic data sharing, disabling, 247-248
  Location Services
   disabling, 245-247
   enabling by app, 247
problem-solving. *See* troubleshooting
purchasing. *See* buying

Q

Qello app, 207
questions, asking Siri, 53
queue (Netflix)
  adding movies/TV shows to, 102
  organizing, 103
  removing movies/TV shows from, 103

R

radio stations
  Beats 1, 197
   listening to, 198
   requesting songs, 199
   show schedule, 197
  curated stations, 199-201
  custom stations
   creating, 201-203
   deleting, 204
  modifying song selections, 203-204
rating
  apps at App Store, 150-151
  Netflix content, 106
reading onscreen text with VoiceOver, 260-261
rebooting. *See* restarting Apple TV
Receiver app, 206

recent apps, accessing, 41

recharging port (remote control), 19

recommendations from Apple Music, 195

improving, 196

redownloading apps, 146

Reduce Loud Sounds feature, 75

reducing

animation/motion of onscreen text, 252-253

transparency of onscreen text, 251

refining searches, 59-60

refunds on apps, 147

Remote app, 46

limitations, 49

setup, 47-48

usage, 48-49

remote control

3D effects, 40

activating sleep mode, 29

Apple TV setup, 20-22

battery

charging, 42, 277

length of charge, 40

low charge level, 42-43

replacing, 42

description, 19

enabling for TV/home theater system control, 26

fast forward/rewind, 39

as game controller, 40

HDMI-CEC support, 27

for multiplayer games, 159

pairing with Apple TV, 33

playing games, 152-153

recent apps, accessing, 41

Remote Loop for, 13-14

restarting Apple TV, 266

Siri, activating, 50

third-party remote controls

editing settings, 36

pairing with Apple TV, 34-35

removing from Apple TV, 37-38

touchpad, adjusting settings, 38

troubleshooting, 277

TV remotes versus, 31-32

TV volume control, 27-28

waking from sleep mode, 29

Remote Loop, 13-14

removing

Apple Music songs from iTunes Music Library, 182-183

apps, 145-146, 149

built-in apps, 149

custom radio stations, 204

movies/TV shows from Netflix queue, 103

third-party remote controls from Apple TV, 37-38

renting

apps, 143

movies via iTunes, 71-73

music. See streaming, music

TV shows via iTunes, 80

replacing remote control battery, 42

requesting songs on Beats 1 radio station, 199

requirements for Apple TV, 7

Apple ID, 8-9

broadband Internet connection, 7

HDMI cable, 8

high-definition TV, 7

resetting

Apple ID password, 274-276

Apple TV, 269-271

cable modem, 279-280

passcodes, 223-224

settings, 223-224

wireless routers, 279

resolution, changing, 234

resources for help, 280
Apple Store, 281, 286
phone support, 286

restarting Apple TV, 265
with remote control, 266
with Settings app, 266
by unplugging, 267

restoring Apple TV, 269-271

results screen (searches), 61-64

reviewing apps at App Store, 150-151

rewind
with remote control, 39
with Siri, 52

routers
resetting, 279
Wi-Fi requirements, 16

S

saving passwords in App Store, 143-145

scores
checking in Game Center, 155
from Siri, 55

screensavers, 239
Apple screensavers, selecting, 240-241
from Photos app, selecting, 242-243
timing for, 243-244

Search app, 25, 60

searching, 56
App Store, 138
within apps, 64
iTunes Music Library, 175
for movies
via HBO apps, 113
via Hulu, 129-130
via iTunes, 68
via Netflix, 101-102
via Showtime apps, 122-123

results screen for, 61-64
with Search app, 25, 60
with Siri, 57-58
refining searches, 59-60
for TV shows
via HBO apps, 113
via Hulu, 129-130
via iTunes, 79-80
via Netflix, 101-102
via Showtime apps, 122-123
universal search, 56-57

Season Pass
buying, 83
getting TV show episodes via, 84

security
Apple ID password, resetting, 274-276
content restrictions, 218
disabling, 222-223
enabling, 219-220
limitations on, 222
managing, 220-222
resetting passcode, 223-224

Seeso, cost of, 97

selecting
onscreen text, enabling high-contrast selectors, 252
screensavers
Apple screensavers, 240-241
from Photos app, 242-243

sending game invitations, 157

settings, 25
accessibility
adjusting zoom levels, 262
changing closed caption style, 256
changing default subtitle language, 259-260
creating custom closed caption style, 257-258
enabling accessibility shortcut, 263

enabling Audio Descriptions, 259

enabling closed captions, 255

reading onscreen text with VoiceOver, 260-261

AirPlay, configuring, 232

audio mode, changing, 236

audio output, changing, 236-237

HDMI output format, changing, 233

interface

changing to bold text, 250

disabling navigation clicks, 253

disabling Siri, 254

disabling sound effects/music, 254

enabling high-contrast selectors, 252

reducing animation/motion, 252-253

reducing transparency, 251

output resolution, changing, 234

privacy

disabling diagnostic data sharing, 247-248

disabling Location Services, 245-247

enabling Location Services by app, 247

limiting ad tracking, 249

resetting, 223-224

restarting Apple TV, 266

screensavers, 239

Apple screensavers, 240-241

from Photos app, 242-243

timing for, 243-244

sleep mode, timing for, 244-245

for third-party remote controls, editing, 36

for touchpad (remote control), adjusting, 38

TV calibration, 235

setup

Apple TV

Ethernet versus Wi-Fi, 16

home theater connections, 17

with iPhone/iPad, 23-24

pairing remote control, 33

ports and connectors, 15-16

with remote control, 20-22

third-party remote controls, 34-35

Remote app, 47-48

sharing diagnostic data, disabling, 247-248

shortcuts, enabling accessibility shortcut, 263

shows. *See* movies; TV shows

Showtime, cost of, 97

Showtime Anytime app

adding items to My List, 123-124

searching, 122-123

signing in, 117-118

watching shows, 124-125

Showtime app

adding items to My List, 123-124

searching, 122-123

signing in, 119-120

subscribing, 120-121

watching shows, 124-125

shuffling music, 189-192

signing in

Apple ID, 272-273

Game Center, 154-155

HBO GO, 108-110

HBO NOW, 110

Hulu, 126-127

iCloud Photos, 212-213

Netflix, 98

network TV apps, 94-97

Showtime Anytime app, 117-118

Showtime app, 119-120

Siri, 50

activating, 50

disabling, 254

enabling movie subtitles, 78

frequently used commands, 51-55

Hulu support, lack of, 132

Remote app and, 49

searching with, 57-58

refining searches, 59-60

Siri button (remote control), 18

Siri Remote by Apple. *See* remote control

skipping songs

on curated radio stations, 201

on custom radio stations, 203

sleep mode

activating with remote control, 29

timing for, 244-245

waking from, 29

slideshows, viewing, 214-215

solving problems. *See* troubleshooting

songs. *See also* music

Apple Music

adding to iTunes Music Library, 180-181

deleting from iTunes Music Library, 182-183

marking as favorite, 188-189

modifying selection on radio stations, 203-204

requesting on Beats 1 radio station, 199

skipping

in curated radio stations, 201

in custom radio stations, 203

sorting app purchases, 147

soundbars, 11-12

connecting to, 17

Sound Check feature, 193-194

sound effects (in navigation), disabling, 254

speakers in home theater system, 11-12

speed of Internet connection, 7

sports scores from Siri, 55

storage management, 148-149

streaming

apps, 148

audio

from iPhone/iPad, 225-227

from Mac, 227-228

games, 148

music, 169. *See also* Apple Music

adding songs to iTunes Music Library, 180-181

canceling Apple Music, 178-179

deleting songs from iTunes Music Library, 182-183

subscribing to Apple Music, 178

streaming services

network TV apps with, 97

Showtime

signing in, 119-120

subscribing, 120-121

style of closed captions

changing, 256

creating, 257-258

subscribing

Apple Music, 178

HBO NOW, 111-112

Hulu, 127-128

Netflix, 99-101

Showtime app, 120-121

subscriptions, 159

managing, 162-163

subtitles. *See* closed captions

surge protectors, 10-11

surround sound systems, 11-12

T

TED app, 134

television. *See* TV

third-party apps, 25

third-party game controllers
  for multiplayer games, 159
  pairing with Apple TV, 45-46
  playing games, 153
third-party remote controls
  editing settings, 36
  pairing with Apple TV, 34-35
  removing from Apple TV, 37-38
time scrubbing
  with remote control, 39
  with Siri, 52
timing
  for screensavers, changing, 243-244
  for sleep mode, changing, 244-245
touchpad (remote control), 17, 32
  3D effects, 40
  adjusting settings, 38
  fast forward/rewind, 39
transparency, reducing onscreen, 251
troubleshooting
  Apple ID
    resetting password, 274-276
    signing in/out, 272-273
  backing up Apple TV, 271
  Internet connection, 278
    resetting cable modem, 279-280
    resetting wireless router, 279
  no picture on TV, 20
  remote control, 277
  resetting/restoring Apple TV, 269-271
  resources for help, 280
    Apple Store, 281, 286
    phone support, 286
  restarting Apple TV, 265
    with remote control, 266
    with Settings app, 266
    by unplugging, 267
  updating tvOS operating system, 267
    automatically, 269
    manually, 268

turning on/off. See disabling; enabling
TV
  calibration settings, 235
  controlling with remote control, 26
  HDMI-CEC support, 27
  TV remotes versus Apple remote
    control, 31-32
  volume control, 27-28
TV shows. See also network TV apps; video
apps
  adding
    to HBO Watchlist, 114
    to My List in Showtime apps, 123-124
    to Netflix queue, 102
  browsing via iTunes, 80-81
  buying
    via iTunes, 82
    Season Pass, 83
  enabling subtitles, 78
  getting Season Pass episodes, 84
  information about, obtaining with Siri,
    52
  organizing in Netflix queue, 103
  rating content in Netflix, 106
  removing from Netflix queue, 103
  searching for
    via HBO apps, 113
    via Hulu, 129-130
    via iTunes, 79-80
    via Netflix, 101-102
    via Showtime apps, 122-123
  watching
    via HBO apps, 115-117
    via Home Sharing, 90-91
    via Hulu, 130-131
    via iTunes, 84, 87
    via Netflix, 104-106
    via Showtime apps, 124-125

tvOS operating system, 14
    updating, 267
        automatically, 269
        manually, 268

U

universal search, 56-57
unplugging Apple TV, 267
updating
    apps, 163-164
    tvOS operating system, 267
        automatically, 269
        manually, 268
uploading photos to iCloud, 212
USB-C port, 15

V

Vevo app, 207
video apps. *See also* movies; TV shows
    Daily Burn, 132
    Funny Or Die, 133
    HBO GO, 107
        adding items to Watchlist, 114
        searching, 113
        signing in, 108-110
        watching, 115-117
    HBO NOW, 107
        adding items to Watchlist, 114
        searching, 113
        signing in, 110
        subscribing to, 111-112
        watching, 115-117
    Hulu, 126
        searching, 129-130
        signing in, 126-127
        subscribing, 127-128
        watching shows, 130-131

MLB.com At Bat, 133
NBA League Pass, 134
Netflix, 98
    adding shows to queue, 102
    organizing queue, 103
    rating content, 106
    removing shows from queue, 103
    searching, 101-102
    signing in, 98
    subscribing to, 99-101
    watching movies/TV shows, 104-106
network TV apps, 93-94
    cable TV and, 94
    signing in, 94-97
    streaming services, 97
Showtime
    adding items to My List, 123-124
    searching, 122-123
    signing in, 119-120
    subscribing, 120-121
    watching shows, 124-125
Showtime Anytime
    adding items to My List, 123-124
    searching, 122-123
    signing in, 117-118
    watching shows, 124-125
TED, 134
WWE Network, 135
YouTube, 135
videos, viewing, 213
viewing
    movies
        via HBO apps, 115-117
        via Home Sharing, 90-91
        via Hulu, 130-131
        information about, 76
        via iTunes, 74-77
        via Netflix, 104-106
        via Showtime apps, 124-125

photos/videos, 213

    with Home Sharing, 215-217

    as slideshow, 214-215

  TV shows

    via HBO apps, 115-117

    via Home Sharing, 90-91

    via Hulu, 130-131

    via iTunes, 84, 87

    via Netflix, 104-106

    via Showtime apps, 124-125

voice control (remote control), 32. *See also* Siri

VoiceOver, enabling, 260-261

volume

  controlling with remote control, 27-28

  of movies, Reduce Loud Sounds feature, 75

  of music, equalizing, 193-194

volume button (remote control), 18

W

waking from sleep mode, 29

warranty on Apple TV, 280

watching. *See* viewing

Watchlist (HBO), adding items to, 114

weather info from Siri, 53-54

Wi-Fi (wireless networking), 16

Windows, AirPlay for, 231

wireless routers, resetting, 279

WWE Network app, 135

X-Z

YouTube app, 135

zoom levels for onscreen text, 262

More Best-Selling **My** Books!

Learning to use your smartphone, tablet, camera, game, or software has never been easier with the full-color My Series. You'll find simple, step-by-step instructions from our team of experienced authors. The organized, task-based format allows you to quickly and easily find exactly what you want to achieve.

Visit quepublishing.com/mybooks to learn more.

REGISTER THIS PRODUCT
SAVE 35%*
ON YOUR NEXT PURCHASE!

How to Register Your Product

- Go to quepublishing.com/register
- Sign in or create an account
- Enter ISBN: 10- or 13-digit ISBN that appears on the back cover of your product

Benefits of Registering

- Ability to download product updates
- Access to bonus chapters and workshop files
- A 35% coupon to be used on your next purchase – valid for 30 days
  To obtain your coupon, click on "Manage Codes" in the right column of your Account page
- Receive special offers on new editions and related Que products

Please note that the benefits for registering may vary by product. Benefits will be listed on your Account page under Registered Products.

We value and respect your privacy. Your email address will not be sold to any third party company.

* 35% discount code presented after product registration is valid on most print books, eBooks, and full-course videos sold on QuePublishing.com. Discount may not be combined with any other offer and is not redeemable for cash. Discount code expires after 30 days from the time of product registration. Offer subject to change.

quepublishing.com